Elder Story 3
Where We Came From

Compiled and Edited by

Gordon A. Long

AIRBORN PRESS

Delta, B. C.

i

ElderStory 3
Where We Came From

Published by

AIRBORN PRESS

4958 10A Ave, Delta, B. C.

V4M 1X8

Canada

ISBN: 978-1-988898-03-2

Printed by CreateSpace

Cover Design by Tania Mendoza
Cover Photo by Cathy Yeulet

Other Books in This Series:

Coming Soon

For the Families

This is a book of real stories about real people. ElderStory has requested that, wherever possible, storytellers get permission from people to use their names and stories. The stories remain the intellectual property of the storytellers. It is our hope and desire that no one will be hurt or offended by his or her portrayal in any of these tales.

For the Storytellers

These stories as published may not be exactly the same as the story you usually tell. It is the nature of folk tales that they change over time. You tell the story differently each time. People remember it differently. In the process of recording/ transcribing/editing, things get changed, especially if there is translation involved. But the story is still your story, and it is a story that people want to hear.

Thanks To

John Lusted and the KinVillage Association in Tsawwassen
Morgan Gadd, for his expertise and support.

Staff, students and families of Ecole Woodward Hill Elementary School, especially Lisa Anderson, Ravinder Grewal, Jas Kooner, Kelly Mcquillan and of course Elaine Vaughan, who organized our sessions.

Staff, students and families of Surrey Central Elementary School, especially principal James Pearce, and Sean Austin, John Kovach, Kevin Larking and Grace Jackson.

Staff and residents at the Langley Lodge Care Home

Pamela Chestnut, Mona, Tania Mendoza and Mercedes at DIVERSEcity.

In Memorium

We would like to dedicate this book to the memory of two of our participants who have passed away since telling us their stories. When you read about their lives in this and other ElderStory books, please take a moment to think of

Maggie Gooderham

Cal Whitehead

and the contributions they have made to Canada over their many years in this country.

Introduction

The ElderStory Project came about in a very natural way. So many people deeply regret not making a record of their family's stories before it was too late. And so those stories died with the people who told them.

Those of us on the Surrey Seniors Planning Table looked for a way to keep family stories moving down through the generations. It is good for children to know where they come from, who their families are. It leads to a sense of belonging and a stronger sense of self worth.

So we sought ways to enhance the telling of stories to keep family members and communities in contact with each other. And the ElderStory Project was born, with the intention of bringing the generations together through storytelling.

Our storytellers come from all walks of life, from all ages, from many cultural groups. Their histories originate in communities in rural Canada: in small villages in India and Iraq: in large towns and big cities around the world. But wherever they originate, the message always comes out the same. "Now we are here, and much though we love the places we came from, in this place we are happy."

The Surrey Seniors' Planning Table and DIVERSEcity Community Resources Society hope that you will enjoy these very Canadian stories.

Contents

ElderStory

Long, long ago and far away there were mountains that stood high and firm.

Through weathering, wind, and rain, frost and heat, part of the mountains broke into thousands of small pieces of stone, rolled and washed away into far-off places, miles and miles away.

These pieces happened to drift and land in British Columbia.

To get to know one another, we started to tell stories about ourselves.

We have passed through hills and valleys, rivers and streams. We saw what we chose to see.

We have come through thunder and storms, sunshine and heat. What we experienced and how we responded were very distinct, because we are all different in shape and size, colour and texture.

Some of us decided to tell everything we experienced throughout our journey. Some chose to share episodes: incidents that impressed us deeply.

This is our story

This is our song

Read the ElderStory books and enjoy.

– Bernadette Law

1.   Coming to Canada

1.   Roslyn Simon – My First Winter

I had always seen snow like in the movies or pictures, in calendars and the like. Having experienced it for the first time was absolutely beautiful. Because the white little fluffy flakes falling on me. I didn't want to take it off my body, my hat or anything. Of course, this was in 1967 and minis were in fashion in New York. We were very fashionable at the time. Everything had to match. So I remember had brown boots, brown leather coat, and my mini dress of course with the tights.

Everything was brown, I remember very well, because a friend took a picture. You couldn't tell the difference between me and the background except for the white snowflakes that happened stick to the wall. But it was a good interesting experience because the snow was so nice and clean. It didn't occur to me that it got absolutely filthy and messy that you have to clean up. Because I picked up and made snowballs and I had them in my pack. I don't know if I expected them to sort of stay and not melt. Then it started to get cold and I'm absolutely freezing.

But it was the most fascinating experience to literally to have it fall on your face and all over you and have you stick your tongue out to catch it but it was a great experience. It's something that I still remember every time I see the snow, and I swear I said, "Don't forget when you saw it the first time, how you're really like a two-year-old playing it.

You know my son, he was born in Canada and of course we went to Trinidad every Christmas. And as soon as we landed back in January, there would be snow in the ground. He would just go and lie in the ground. He really loved it. It was a good experience. It was something that quite memorable, 40 years later.

2.   Bernadette Law – Cultural Differences.

For the first day of drawing class, I had my pencils, 2-B and 4-B and 6-B and so on, so I'd make nice drawings. But I still made a mistake. So I wanted to rub it off. So I didn't have something to rub it off with. So I look at the student next to me, and it's a guy, and I say timidly and very softly, " Can you lend me your rubber?"

1

And he says loudly, "What do you want my rubber for?" Finally I found out that here it's called an eraser.

After the first year of art school, I got a job with the art centre to teach arts and class Saturday morning and afternoon, and in the evening the Calgary Continuing Education hired me to teach watercolour and oil painting and acrylic painting to adults. So I still went to school but when I went home it was so dark, I rented a basement and the entrance was at the back, and I had to feel my way. The next day I talked to the landlady. "It's so dark when I come home, especially going to my room in the basement. Can you lend me a torch?"

And she said, "Are you going to burn my house?"

I said, "No, I just need to borrow a torch. I'll buy one on Saturday when I have time, but I go to school in the morning and I teach at night."

So there are so many different meanings to words. We call it "lift," but here it's "elevator." We call it "clark," but here they say, "clerk." And there's so many different kind of things.

When I went to teach at night, I used to be an Art teacher in an elementary school. As a teacher in Hong Kong, you are very highly respected, and in the morning the students and the parents when they saw me, they stop and say, "Good morning, Miss Law." And here they call me by my first name. I did a lot of work and painting in China, and I felt uncomfortable with being called by my first name.

But after some time I got used to it, and I like it, because in Hong Kong when you are a teacher, you are the model for perfection. No matter where you go you have to act like a teacher, and you are like a walking dictionary. You should know everything. So if someone asks you something and you don't have an answer, you have to try to think of something to tell them. But here, I don't have to do that. If I don't know something, I can say, "Sorry, I don't have the answer, but I'll tell you next week. "

And they say, "Okay," and it's acceptable.

In Hong Kong the teacher is on the platform high above model for everyone, but now I feel I'm just a human being. I can make mistakes and they will accept it. So one day a student of mine phoned me and said, "I came down with a bad cold and I can't come to class."

And I said, "That's good. Take care of your cold, and come back to class when you're better.

And she said, "How can you say something like that to me?"

"I said, "What have I said wrong?"

"When I told you I was sick, and then you said, 'That's good.' You shouldn't say something like that. You should have said, 'That's fine.'"

"But don't 'that's fine' and 'that's good' mean the same thing?"

She said, "No, no, it doesn't mean the same thing. And after some time I learned that 'fine' and 'good' are different, and at different times you say things in a different way."

I read in the Calgary Herald that a tourist came to Calgary and he rented a car and drove downtown, and he found an empty lot and parked the car there and walked around the city. After an hour he came back and he got a parking ticket. And he was so mad, and he said, "Why did they give me a parking ticket?" And he remembered that while he was walking he saw the courthouse. So he went there and said, "Why did you give me a parking ticket?"

They said, "Where did you park?"

He said, "I parked in an empty lot. There was a sign that said, 'Fine for parking,' so I parked there. Why did they give me a ticket?" So finally he didn't have to pay for the parking ticket, but the owner of the property was asked to change the sign.

I came here about 50 years ago, and at that time China was not open, and a Chinese guy went to the Vancouver International Airport and wanted to buy a ticket to Red China.

They said, "No, we can't sell you a ticket."

He said, "Why not?"

They said, "You can't go there."

"I came from there. My family, my wife and my children are waiting for me. I have to go back."

"No, no, no, you can't go back. There's no ticket to go to China."

He said, "I came from there. I came to Vancouver to work. Now I want to go home."

And they said, "No."

At that time, the Chinese people carry a basket, a rattan basket, not a briefcase, and he put this on the counter and opened it, and he said, "Look. I've got money."

And it was all small change, one dollar and ten dollars five dollars and coins. And he said, "I've got money. Why can't you sell me the ticket?"

They said, "No, no, we can't sell you the ticket, because China is red, because it's communist." So they said, "No, you can't go there."

So they got the department head to talk to him, and after a long talk finally they found out that he didn't want to go to Red China. He wanted to go to Regina, in Saskatchewan. So because he was Chinese, when he said he wanted to go home, they assumed he meant Red China.

But they don't even think about that. So that's my story for today.

3.   Sue Murguly - Refugee

If it wasn't for my parents, I wouldn't be a refugee. Basically it started – and I'll just take it back a little ways – one evening when my Dad comes rushing into our house and says, "There's a revolution against the Russians."

The next thing I know is he goes rushing out and then he comes back in and he has a rifle in his hand. And I'm looking at my Dad, like, "What are you doing? You don't know anything about guns."

And he's all excited.

The next thing I know about it is that a Russian tank shows up in our village of about ten thousand people. And that one tank proceeds to break down in the middle of our town square. So there's this tank, off its treads, and it can't do anything. So we just stand around and mock it for a while until we get tired of it.

Then weird things start to happen because of the Russians. We only get lights at night every other day. So I just hate the feeling of having blacked out lights, the place being dark. I don't know why, I just hated that.

And then, all of a sudden one day, we left home. I know we crossed the border on the 21st, and I know we went one day on the train, and then we stayed a farm another day, so we probably left our home on the 19th of December 1956. By then the Russians had come back into Hungary,

In between Nov 23 and when the Russians came back into Hungary on November 4 they basically they took back everything in Hungary at that time.

I do remember hearing a Hungarian radio station pleading for Americans to come and help, come and help, come and help. And they didn't because of Suez. We timed our revolution wrong, because the Suez Canal crisis was going on at the same time.

So my parents came and told us that night, the night before we were to leave, that we were going to leave. They hadn't told us because they didn't want anyone else to know. We were to say that we were going to our grandparents' place, and we were taking the train from Balaton to Vestremon, a bigger town than we were in.

We got off the train and stayed there one night, in the city, in somebody's house. And then we went on foot to a farm the next night. We went outside the big town and walked to a farm where we were taken to wait for the cover of night. I remember the terrain. Some parts of it were sloped. We walked, I would say, at least two hours or three hours. So we basically stayed in that farm and then crossed during the evening.

We were waiting with a whole bunch of people, at least 10 of us. I didn't know these other people. Just my Mum and Dad and my sister. The rest were all strangers.

We waited for nighttime, and then we started out from there, walking. There was snow on the ground until we got to a river. It wasn't the crossing at Andau, because that had a bridge. Dad said it wasn't a good place because I remember that. I don't think there was a boat there, just a little rowboat that took you across. It wasn't a huge journey. The rowboat was just big enough to get across.

I remember stopping there and saying, "How can a tiny little river like this separate one country from another?" I was 9 years old. And when I was across on the other side, I said, "Are we in Austsria?" and my my Mum and Dad said, "Yes."

And I just whooped out. I went, "Yippee!"

And they went, "Shh! We're not safe yet."

That was a real awakening for me.

There were trucks waiting for us. It was well organized, because we were almost the last of the refugees to come out of Hungary. So the surge of refugees that came out of Hungary probably started in November, because the Russians came back and so then the Hungarians said, "That's it. We're outta here. We're scared." Some of them were identifiable for their part in the revolution.

But Mum and Dad, I have no idea why they waited that long, but they did wait. There were border patrols. You had to know where to cross. You couldn't just go anywhere. My parents had a guide that led us from that farmhouse. Then the last train station we actually had somebody that led us to the safe house, before we went to the farmhouse. We had help from that point on. Dad paid ahead of time for these people.

I was really aware of my life, even as a little kid. I was always aware of what was happening. There was money exchanged between my Dad and this man, and I sort of figured out that they were there to help us.

Then when we landed up in the house and saw that other people were there, they came there not out of serendipity, but they all had the same help. Then when the man led us out, I knew that he was helping us get to the border.

I you tried it by yourself your chances of being caught were really high. And communication would have been difficult. We didn't have telephones in Hungary at that time. You wrote letters. We did not have sophisticated communications, and that's probably why it took so long for us to leave Hungary. My Dad was probably setting it all up.

We weren't carrying very much. Just a small suitcase like I was going to visit Grandma. I carried it myself. Mum was carrying some lunch. I remember she killed my chicken. That was the first time that I had fried chicken. So she fried up my chicken. It was called Bubos, because it had a little hump on its head. That's what a hump is, a bub.

I knew that I was eating my chicken, and at first I tried to be really sad until I tasted it, and then I started really enjoying that chicken, because I didn't get that kind of food very much.

4.   Sue Murguly – In Austria

This truck was already waiting for us. It was an army truck with wooden sides and benches inside to put people on. When we arrived they quickly made us get on the truck. They realized the incredible small distance between one bank and the other of the river. They weren't stupid, and neither was I.

They loaded us up and took off with us. We arrived sat this facility, and it was filled with Red Cross personnel, and I think some nuns. They had their weird outfits on, anyway. They gave us rum tea, because it was so cold. It was the middle of winter, so they were very worried about us catching a cold or getting sick.

It was the cleanest facility I've ever seen. My Mum kept a clean house, but this was so clean. The sheets were just totally white, and each bed had an army-type blanket on it. So we were able to sleep. Every one of us got a bed. They were bunk beds, only two tiered.

I think it wasn't a big building. It seemed like a lower, camp-type place. That was where we spent the first night, and then we were transferred to another place further away from the border. The second place where we stayed was a dance hall. All we had was straw mattresses. It was ornately decorated, almost like a bordello. Basically, I remember we got a spot – because Mum was always pushy – right on the stage. So we had a little bit of elevation. But my Mum got quite ill, and she probably pretended to be more ill than she was, because she was very dramatic about it.

I do think that she got penicillin shots, because I think they felt that her cold was worse than just a cold. She could have had pneumonia, but I don't think so. You don't get over pneumonia in two or three days.

That's where we stayed. At that time, it was interesting because of the way that they set out the feeding facilities. You actually stayed in the building, and you couldn't leave. All your needs were met within the building, and one of them was food. It's the first time that I've ever used a tray to gather up food. I can't remember what I ate, but obviously it was fine with me. We did use the middle of the hall to play as kids.

I think at that time one of the places, they had Saint Nicholas or some sort of Santa Claus because it was Christmas time; they had a Saint Nicholas come to visit with us. It was very Austrian. They had a weird tradition, different from Hungarians, and I think it was at that dance hall that I received my first gift. They did give us amazing clothing, because we weren't dressed for the Austrian winter. They gave us boots, and some warm pants and warm coats and warm sweaters and gloves and hats and stuff like that, so it was pretty amazing.

They had a contest where I won something. I know it was a doll, in a little carrier. And I was just so excited. I don't know why I won, I think it was some question I had to answer and I got it right, and I won.

When these wonderful Austrians saw the look on all the other girls' faces, when I won, the next day they showed up with dolls for every girl in the group. Wasn't that sweet? Then I could play with them, because they had their dolls and I had mine. I didn't care. The fact that I got the first one was all that was important to me.

5.   *Sue Murguly – Christmas in Austria*

They brought all sorts of Christmas things in for us. There were things like chocolate every day, sometimes twice a day, great big slabs of it. What I found was how well looked after we were. I can't believe that there wasn't any –well maybe from my Mum and Dad's perspective there might have been missteps, but not from mine. I thought we were really looked after well. There was enough food, there was consideration, but we didn't stay in that place that long, maybe three or four days at the very most.

Then we were transferred to a camp near Heiming. There, they had army barracks. They had rows of army barracks. At first it was just a everybody just got a bunk, and then my mother noticed that four young ladies who did not have children had a cabin all to themselves, so you know, my mother being my mother, she said "I think the cabins should be given to two families with children, instead of single women. Why should they get the privilege?"

So that's what happened. My family moved in with another couple who had no children. So there were six of us in the cabin.

We stayed there quite a while. Practically until the beginning of spring. We didn't go to school. All we did was there was this wonderful mountain with a waterfall on it that was frozen, and we would go up into the top of that and we would squat down and slide on our hobnailed boots and come shwooshing down. My sister broke her nose because she took a tumble and banged her nose on the ice.

There was a priest, and he did set up some sort of school or some activity centre for the youth. We put on a musical. And I got the leading part. I used to have a picture of it. There was very rich girl who wanted the prince, and then the poor maiden, and I was the poor maiden, and I got my prince. I can still sing some of the songs from that play.

In the spring one time we went up to Vienna because we had to apply for refugee status. The Canadian Embassy sent a delegation to sign up people who wanted to come to Canada. The Canadians were the only ones that sent a delegation to expedite our applications so we didn't have to go and stand in line. They did all the official business right there at the camp. So we had to go to Vienna to get our papers, and Mum and Dad brought all of our documentation: our birth certificates and that.

When they got to Vienna my parents found out that they could apply to all sorts of places, but the borders were closing very quickly, and USA wasn't taking any more, so their choice was either to go to Brazil or Canada. My Mum said, "I'm not going to Brazil." My Dad had Austrian background, so he wanted to go to Brazil because there were a lot of Germans there, but they decided on Canada.

From Vienna we were taken to this place close to the airport. We stayed there until a flight could be arranged for us. And then away we came.

6.   Sue Murguly – In the Camp.

I loved the camp life.

I remember sitting on the top bunk and this woman trying to run a séance just over the wall. We were just totally waiting for those chairs to move. And my Mum was mumbling that this was all nonsense, because she was very religious.

Even as a child at 9 years old I realized just the incredible kindness of the Austrians and the incredible organization. Yes we were in camps just like today's refugees, but I think it was better organized. But there weren't as many refugees as we have now.

All of Hungary is grateful to Austrians for letting us cross into their country. I mean, we had an empire together until the First World War, so there was a connection. Hungary still has a wonderful border relationship with Austria now, with free crossing.

7.   George Murguly – The Hungarian Revolution

A brief history before we leave.

The Hungarian Revolution started October 23 1956, and it was successful for about 10 days against the Russians, because the occupying forces weren't interested in fighting. But on November 4 the Russian Army invaded with a series of tanks, and occupied the country and put the revolution down. That was in November.

So my Dad decided to leave Hungary. We lived in a town about 10 km outside Budapest. I remember we boarded the train to go to Budapest to catch the trans-country train to the west to Austria, and that was the way we were planning to escape. We boarded the night train – this was about mid-November – going west, and we went to a border town next to the Austrian border, disembarked, and joined a group of fellow-refugees who were going to cross the border. It was all rolling countryside, a lot of trees. There was no fence at the border, just a wide clearing through the woods.

After WWII the border was mined, but the mines were in the ground for about ten years, and before the revolution they decided to pull the mines up. So when we crossed the border wasn't mined. It was just a swath through the trees. We got to the border and the Border Patrol caught us, the whole group. They escorted us back into town, but there were so many of us the jail couldn't hold us, so what they decided to do was send us to jail in Budapest, so the Hungarian soldiers, operating under Russian rule, forced us on the train, and we headed back toward Budapest.

The train was full, and some of the people knew the train's comings and goings, and they said, "At the next corner the train will have to slow down to make the corner."

So my father and I – it was just the two of us, my mother stayed behind; she had diabetes – we jumped off the train as it went around the curve, and headed back toward the border, walking.

By this time we had figured out the time schedule of the border patrol. So the exact same spot as we were before, we managed to get to the border, walking from the town, and got across without being caught.

We entered Austria, and the Austrians were waiting. They were waiting for the refugees. So we crossed into Austria and managed to get to a road, and the Austrians picked us up with a truck and took us to the nearest town and put us up in a big building, maybe an old school house or something. They had iron beds and put us up for the night, fed us. I said, "Finally I get some holidays."

Next morning my father stuck me in an Austrian school, they all speaking German. I didn't know a word, because in Hungary the official language was Hungarian, and the second was Russian. So I had a little bit of Russian, but I didn't know any German, and there I was, trying to gather my wits about in a class.

And this lasted about a week, and my father decided to go to England. Immediately they packed us up and put us on a train to the English Channel. We went through Germany.

When we had gone through Budapest, I saw the damage done by the Russian tanks to the city. They shot it all to pieces during the revolution. What was fascinating about Germany was that everything was new and rebuilt since WW II.

We got to the English Channel, and got a boat, and I remember getting a little seasick, and we crossed the channel. It was a rough crossing, and went to London. What was amazing about London was that London had not recovered from WWII. There were still bombed out lots and whole blocks in ruins, and everything else. That was what I remember.

I said, "Oh, boy, time for holidays."

Next day, bang, I'm in school. An English school in the middle of London. I remember we stayed in a place called Wapping next to the Thames. It was an old military hospital. The only thing I remember, we stayed three months, and the English were very good to us. They took all the kids on tours around the city, to see Buckingham Palace, the Tower of London, the Crown Jewels, and I still have a memory –

and this was mostly the Red Cross did all this – they took us all these kids on these tours, Piccadilly Circus, and they fed us ice cream in these little Dixie cups, vanilla ice cream with a wooden spoon. I ate so many of them I can't even look at one of those.

We stayed in London and Dad was very versatile. He was a machinist, the last job he had. He had other jobs besides. He was a schoolteacher at one time and an accountant another time. He got a job in London right away. He didn't speak a word of English, but he could read a blueprint. So he was a lathe operator. So he went to work, I went to school.

I remember just highlights from the school. There I was, a dazed Hungarian in an English school, picking up words here and there, and I saw the boxing team. So I signed up for the boxing team. Boxing was very popular in schools in London at the time. They put me in the ring, with no instructions, nothing. They just put me in with a guy and he pummelled the sxxt out of me. I said, "This is it. I'm not doing any boxing. There's gotta be some other more pleasant way of spending your time."

And then we left London. My Dad decided he was not going to stay in England; he was going to go to Canada. He never told me why. When you're an 11-year-old you just follow. After three months in London we moved to a place called Buxton, which was a resort town, and they put us up in a spa hotel. It was a spa place, and I said, "Holidays again."

Next day, I'm in school. The highlight of the whole visit was my Dad and I walked the countryside, and there were these old fortress towers on the hilltops, and we walked to some of them and looked around, and I remember getting into trouble at the hotel. It was something like a five-storey hotel, and very plush, with velvet upholstery and everything else. I remember two of us kids went up in the attic and climbed out on the roof. Some of the windows came through the roof, and we were going to peek in to find out what was going on inside, and we got caught.

Of course everybody five storeys below was waving, "Come down!"

I got in a lot of trouble over that.

Our big outing was that an American Captain, of the Air Force, I think, decide to come by and give us a tour of the countryside. I can't remember so much where we drove, but he took us to the dog races. I'd never seen anything like it. I didn't know what dogs were for, I was just staring at all these dogs running around following the rabbit. The American family was very nice to us.

We left England after three months of that. So our total stay in England was six months. Three months in London and three months in Buxton, which was in the countryside. Then we flew and I remember this was all paid by the Canadian government, from England to Canada, to Gander. We landed in Gander and refueled, and I think we landed in Montreal. They put us on the train. My father wanted to go to Vancouver, because he had been a prisoner of war in WWII and he froze his feet, so he was afraid of cold. It was the middle of winter in Canada, and it was very cold, and he said, "The climate is much nicer on the West Coast."

So we decided to come to Vancouver, and the Canadian Government put us on the train, 5 days across Canada from Montreal to Vancouver, and we arrived in Vancouver and they put us up in an immigration building right on the waterfront. Big red building about three storeys high provided with bunk beds and everything else, and they fed us and kept us there for a couple of days and then we went to Abbotsford to the old airport, which was no longer in use at the time, but all the Air Force barracks were still useable.

So they put us up in the Air Force barracks. There were several hundred refugees. I think we stayed two months. I remember going through the swamps and rafting through them. I had no school. I finally got my holidays.

Then, at the beginning of the summer we moved into Vancouver. Now this is really interesting. You have to remember we just escaped the Russians who overtook Hungary and shot it to pieces, and we went to Vancouver and we were put up by a Russian man who had a house – this was all subsidized by the Canadian Government – who put us up as refugees and looked after us and gave us a room and bedding and furniture and everything else, and this was a Russian. He was actually Ukrainian, but still. Just the other side of the story. Because you're Russian, you're not just a soldier, there are other people around as well.

My father went to work in a sawmill, and he was physically not a strong man, and he just couldn't handle the physical work in the sawmill. Just hauling planks wasn't going to work, and logging wasn't going to work.

So he decided, and he was an educated man, and he started picking up the language, and he decided he would go back to school, and the Canadian Government took care of that and he went to Vancouver Vocational Institute, which later on became BCIT. He took drafting. He didn't want any physical work. He did very well. He was a very bright man. I've seen some of his work, and he's really bright and he learned a lot of engineering as well, besides drafting. So it wasn't just drawing that he learned. So there was a lot of engineering theory that he learned as well, which I discussed with him years later when I became an engineer.

So he passed and then in the fall I started school in the local school right next to where we lived. We lived on the east side of town. Not the best part, but anyway...

My family was Catholic, so I went to Sacred Heart School, which was primarily catering to the Italians in Vancouver.

My father finished the vocational school and became a draftsman, and his English was improving, but you have to remember when you're a technical guy, you don't need much English. Just technical words. The instructor picked him up and took him all around town to the suitable companies until he got a job. The instructor did that. And he got a job with Alcan in their extrusion plant in Richmond. Alcan makes aluminum in Kitimat and ships it down to Vancouver where they warm up the ingot and push it through a die and make window frames and door frames and ship masts and everything else.

The Richmond plant is closed, now. It closed soon after my father retired.

So he had a steady job, I was going to school, and in the meantime we were still involved in the Hungarian circles in Vancouver. Originally we used the German church for services, and then eventually the Hungarians got together and bought their own church on the East Side of Vancouver. So this is Catholic.

I went to school. I finished. They were really good to me at the Elementary School, because I was 12 years old by the time I started at Sacred Heart, and they held me for a year and saw that I was great in Math and Sciences and had lots of trouble with English, so they skipped me two grades to put me up with my own age level. So I finished Grade 8 in Sacred Heart and started High School in Notre Dame, which was also on the East Side of Vancouver. In the meantime we joined the Hungarian community. My father helped form the Hungarian Boy Scouts in Vancouver. It was ethnic, but it was fine.

And the years passed, and during the final years of my high school at one of the Hungarian activities, a ball, I met Sue, and then the story goes on.

8. Mohammed Rafiq – Coming to Canada

I did my Master's in Botany in 1965. My father around that time was suffering from cancer. He was very sick, and after about four years of dealing with cancer he passed away in '65. I was saddened by that, and on top of that there was a war between India and Pakistan. All the jobs were frozen, and though I had a Master's degree I was not finding any jobs. But I wanted to patriotically to do my job in Pakistan, and be part of the community, but I was not finding any job in my own profession.

So I found some odd jobs in the meantime. I was a medical representative for a few months, trying to sell medicines. Then after that for about a year I was a research associate with one of the botanists over there. From there on, I was seeing that I was not getting settled, and my elder brother who had come to the States first. He was an MD from Pakistan. He came to the States, and he started out training as a neurosurgeon, but he did not like that, so from there he moved to Montreal to Royal Victoria Hospital, and started doing his internship as well as his Master's in surgery from McGill at the same time.

That is when I decided that I should migrate to where he was and carry on from there. Interestingly I was posted in Rawalpindi near Islamabad, which is where the Canadian Immigration office was. One day I decided to go and see an immigration officer over there. I had an appointment, and he interviewed me. He asked me what do I do?

I told him that I had done my Masters in Botany.

He told me, "We don't need any basic scientists. We have plenty of botanists in Canada."

I was just about to leave the room, but he called me back. "What else do you do these days?"

I told him that I was a medical representative.

"Why didn't you say that you are a chemical salesman? I can recommend you as a chemical salesman to come to Canada."

I said, "Whatever you want to say is fine with me. I just want to go to Canada."

14

So that is how I got my immigration selection. Then going through all the other procedures. Going through the medical and things like that.

I landed in Montreal in March of 1969, where my brother was. He was going to be there finishing his Masters in two or three months, and he was coming to Vancouver.

So those two or three months I'm glad I had some support, because he gave me some money and opened an account for me, I think it was four or five hundred dollars.

He told me, "Enjoy yourself while you are here."

He had also rented an apartment for me, too, so I was very lucky to have his support.

After he had finished his Masters both of us drove from Montreal to Vancouver and he started his internship here in VGH and I got admitted at UBC in the Botany Department. My research was in marine yeast but in that direction I found a job in the Ministry of Environment in the vegetation ecologist and I started doing that.

9.   *Graham Mallett – Travel to England*

I ended up doing my teaching education, taught school in Sydney for four and a half years. Then I decided I wanted to travel, so I sold my car and bought a ticket on a ship to England. Then I decided to change that, and decided to get off the ship in Italy and travel overland.

When I got to Egypt I thought, "it's pretty interesting here," so I got off the ship there and I travelled around Egypt for a little bit. Went to Cairo. Then I caught a plane to Beirut and stayed there for three weeks, travelled around the Middle East a bit. I went to Jerusalem; it was in Jordan then.

Then I was headed towards London; I planned to take a school so after a while in Beirut I caught a train to Istanbul and took a train up through Syria, which took three days. I had a third class ticket on wooden seats, and to get food the train would stop in villages and people would come and sell you fresh tomatoes and things like that. You could get out and get some water and cream and that kind of thing.

We got to Istanbul. I seem to remember I caught a bus across to Greece, then I hitchhiked all the way down through Greece and caught a boat over to Brindisi in Italy, and hitchhiked all the way up to Brussels, and then a ferry to England.

10.   Jamilla – Jobs in Iraq and Canada

I am Jamilla. I have one boy and one girl. I came from Iraq in 2010. I am a citizen of Canada now. My daughter is 24 years old. My son is 22. My daughter is studying Pharmacy, and she works in the airport. My son is working at the Surrey Mazda dealership.

I was born in Ninevah. I have three other brothers and one sister. All of them are passed away; it is just me here. I finished High School in Iraq and I worked in the Ministry of Trade for 30 years, in Accounting. Now I am applying for a job, but no one has called me for a job. I don't have a certificate for that. You have to study here to get a certificate, and apply for a job. It is the same system of accounting here, but I have a problem with the language. I have to study.

11.   Prince Singh – My Family Coming to Canada

One day maybe about 22 or 23 years ago some of my father's family had come to Canada. The way this happened was my grandmother's Mom had died here in Canada. At the time you had to have a visa to enter Canada, so they wouldn't let my grandmother through. So they wouldn't let her board the plane, and she was sitting in India, and they had to postpone the funeral to wait until my grandma could come. My grandma's brothers were going back and forth trying to get her the visa. Finally they got a visa, but it was only a temporary visa for two weeks, so she came, but then the day she came they went straight to the City Hall and got her a year's visa. So she stayed here.

My Dad stayed with his sister and brother-in-law in India. When my Grandma came, she became a citizen, and eventually, because if you're a citizen and your child lives in another country you can get him a visa right away. So she got him a visa. Then when he got his citizenship, he met my Mum and they got married.

2. Life Overseas

1.   *Maggie Gooderham – Before the War in England*

My father was a brewer. He was in the First War: 1914 to 1919, the whole of the war. He was in the trenches all the time, and his poor legs were all black from being in the trenches for that long.

He was a wonderful man. I loved him dearly. I had one sister, two years older than me. My maiden name was Fitzgerald. He was an Irishman. He came from a fairly large family. They were all so nice.

But he was not happy with my mother. She was not right for him. She was English, and quite different. He was a typical Irishman. Lots of fun and very social. She was quite the opposite, which was a shame. They didn't get on at all. They really should have divorced, but in those days people didn't do that, so we all had an unhappy childhood, really. She was not nice to him at all. She was always grumbling to me about him, and he never retaliated, which he should have done. He let her get away with all these awful things she said about him. Because looking back I would have stood up for him more, but when you're that age you don't understand these things. She was so unkind to him, and I so regretted later in life that I hadn't been more on his side, as it were. I didn't understand at the time.

So that was that.

We lived in a town, in Guildford. It was quite small in those days, of course. It's hard to imagine. We had no cars or anything. We had to put our cars up on blocks in the garage. We had the distributor cap somewhere different in case the Germans had access to a bunch of cars, because they couldn't drive without the distributor cap.

It seems strange, now, to have no cars. My sister and I – it sounds silly – we loved our car. We had a Daimler, and it was up on blocks, so she and I used to sit in the back and play cards, because we liked being in the car. It sounds silly, but at the time we liked it.

People didn't realize quite how close we came to losing the war, you know. They'd taken over the whole of Europe, and Greece and Norway, and most of North Africa.

I remember Dunkirk. After that, in England everybody expected to be invaded, and they would walk right over us. My dear father joined the Home Guard and they used to drill with broomsticks.

17

Nobody had any weapons of any kind in the country. They could have walked right in. But Hitler made that stupid mistake of invading Russia instead. It was absolutely idiotic.

And Dunkirk. At the time we regarded it as a great victory, because a call came out over the BBC, "Would anyone with a small boat go to Dunkirk, and help to rescue everyone that made their way to the beach at Dunkirk?" So all these little boats made their way to Dunkirk, and they picked about 300,000 men, which at the time we thought was a huge victory, which it was, but it was a big defeat. At the time, rescuing all these Poles and French and English, to us it seemed wonderful.

I remember my mother coming up to us and saying, they had this thing that the church bells would all ring if the invasion started. And one night she came up to us and said to my sister and me. "Get up girls, the invasion has started." Of course it seemed at the time as if it was so possible. We got up and packed a case of absolute nonsense. Nothing useful. Photographs and useless things. Then we went downstairs and listened to the radio, and it must have been a false alarm. But at the time it seemed so desperately real. It was frightening, because at the time it was so believable. Which it was, of course.

But if it ever happened again I wouldn't go out on the road. I'd die in bed. It seems a much better idea. Of course we don't know at the time.

When the school decided to evacuate to the country, my parents didn't want me to go. So I took a secretarial course. My parents were okay with that. It was something I could do that I could work with.

2.   *Mohammed Rafiq – Life in Pakistan*

My name is Mohammed Rafiq. I was born in India in 1945. I don't think the date of birth is important, but my date of birth is not quite correct the way it has been written in the papers. Hardly anybody from those days has an accurate date. There are no records. Being busy in his job, my Dad sent us with somebody to go to school, and whatever the teacher wanted, he put as the date of birth. My elder brother's date of birth is the first of April, which he regrets. Someone reminds him that he's an April Fool.

My family migrated to Pakistan in 1949. My father was an overseer in the Irrigation Department in India. He had a very respectable job. When he migrated we had to leave everything in India and walk all the way to Pakistan, and at the border town of

Lahore, where we stayed in the refugee camp for two or three weeks if I remember it right.

My father found a job it a remote town at the edge of Beluchistan, but part of Punjab, which was called Deraghazikhan. Where most of the community was Beluchis, speaking a different language, which was Seraiki.

We grew up there, and I started my schooling there, and after my early schooling my sister lived in Lahore, and my brothers and I all went to Lahore for higher education. I did my Bachelor of Science in Biology in the Government College of Lahore, which is a very reputable college. From there I went on to do a Masters of Science in Botany in the Punjab University.

From there I migrated to Canada in 1969 when I was about 24 or 25. One of the reasons was that I had some support from my elder brother who was a medical student who was doing his internship at the Royal Victoria Hospital in Montreal, and he gave me some support and then I came to Canada.

He luckily had his final year of residence here at Vancouver General, and I, having done my Masters, wanted to have some more education and research, and I joined UBC in the Botany Department, and I went for my second Masters Degree as a Graduate Student. I did that, and in that time, I was hired by the Ministry of Environment of British Columbia as an ecologist. I worked with them for almost 30 years, and retired here.

And in that direction I had some international involvement as an environmental scientist in the study of tsunami research. I did that and I went to various places and gave talks about the science of environmental protection, and mostly costal environmental protection and various possibilities in there.

Then I retired about 2000, and I am enjoying my retirement, and giving as best as I can to the community. My own community from Pakistan, and also the community at large, from whom I have learned a lot.

3.   *Kartar Singh Meet − My Place in the Family*

We have a social event during the month of July, which lasts for 15 days. My aunt was carrying my elder brother on her shoulder and crossing a pool of water, walking over a tree trunk. Her foot slipped and the boy fell down, drowned and died. In the family, then, I was fourth in succession amongst siblings, but eldest among three brothers. That got me special and preferable treatment.

4. Kartar Singh Meet – In Search of Excellence

I started school at about 6. In India, entry age to school is 6 years. I was in a government school but it was run by the District Education Board. It was known as District Board Primary School. It was just a mud house, basically made from local sources. There were no windows, no electricity, no facilities. We used to walk about 5 miles every day. There was only one teacher for all 4 classes. He taught all of the classes diligently and honestly, and the level of education in those days was much better. We were taught the 20 x 20 multiplication table at primary school, and the multiplication table of 1.5 times, 2.5 times, 3.5 times and 4.5 times, all memorized.

The interesting thing is that I was one of the intelligent kids. So at about ten years old I was sent for a competitive exam to get the Government Scholarship. That means knowledge-wise, school knowledge and book knowledge is okay. I could have competed earlier, but I had never left my village in the rural area before that.

I went to appear in the competitive exam. I was taken to a very big hall, the like of which I had never seen in my village. I was wearing a shirt and pajamas of coarse multi-layered cloth and straight dark colors. I didn't know what to do. I had developed a sort of fear psychosis and I started urinating in my pajamas. For the 3-hour duration of the exam I sat there and wrote my exam and urinated in my pajamas in trickles, and by the time the exam was over I was all wet. That was the horrible experience I had at primary school level. But I did pass the exam.

But then I went to high school, because in India they usually had a primary school up to grade 4, then middle school up to grade 8 and high school up to grade 10. Then I was a student of 5th class, I was intelligent and my IQ was fairly high. My father taught me English from whatever he had learned in the British Indian Army. Compared to other children, I was better off.

Then I got selected by the school to appear in a High School Scholarship Examination. Now I was the only student from my school. And if a teacher had to accompany me to the District Headquarters, which was 70 miles from my village, I would have to pay his expenses.

My school said, "It may not be viable for you or possible for us to give him money to take you for that competitive exam. But there is a Government Middle School in the neighbouring village that sends its students every year for the competitive exam. You can be sent with them."

That school sent 3 boys and a teacher that year, 1955. So my school coordinated with them and I accompanied that teacher to the District Headquarters. Since there were 3 students and 1 teacher and there were only 2 beds, I slept on the ground in a small room. And believe you me, although there were 3 students, only 1 of them got the scholarship, and I was the first student of my school to win a scholarship and bring honor to my school. I got the scholarship of 6 rupees per month, whereas my dad's pension was 19 rupees per month. So it was in those days my scholarship amounted to 30% of my dad's pension, which he earned with 23 years of military service.

I went to grade 9 as a regular student with a merit scholarship from the government.

So I urinated in my pajamas at grade 4 level, and 4 years thereafter I got a merit scholarship from the government. I think it's a big jump for me.

5. *Kartar Singh Meet – Love Life*

My point is, I didn't know what love is. But since I was a precocious child when I stepped into adolescence, I too felt as if I was looking for love. In rural India on average, to think of having any love or relationship or saying falling in love naturally with anybody, one just can't think of it. Everybody at that age is a poet or a lover whether it's a boy or a girl.

When I was in high school I had a neighbour, the wife of one of our village schoolteachers. She was the second wife of the teacher, because his first wife had died. The teacher was in his late 30s. She must have been in her late teens, maybe 17 or 18. To me she looked so beautiful that I fell in so-called love with her. Her name was Meeto. Therefore, I adopted a pet name, Meet, so that I could write poems addressed to her as Meet. I started writing, and that is how a poet was born. I could never talk to her. I could only just see her and be happy. Because our society in India in those days didn't permit that sort of affair, and to fall in love with the wife of somebody else was a sin.

But I was so innocent, so lovelorn, not knowing what love is. I just felt fascinated by that female and the poet was born.

I was actually engaged to another girl when I was a student in the second grade. We continued to be engaged for almost 9 years. I wanted to study and her parents wanted an early marriage, so it didn't materialize. They got the girl married to another person.

Actually I wanted to be a teacher. But since my father was a soldier, he gave me an option.

He said, "Either you join me in agriculture," – which was his profession after retirement – "or join the Indian Army." And I went and joined the Army. I used to write poems, of course. Whatever about, I don't know; I can't remember them.

Then I married my wife – we have been married for 56 years now, and celebrated it last month – and we had our first child. Her level of education is primary, which means she studied only to grade level 4.

Then there was a major setback for me. The 26th of January 1962 when I took my wife to a cantonment, which was Army Forces Base. It was raining and she was just sobbing.

I asked her, "What is the problem?"

She said, "You have married me and you have a daughter, but you still continue to write poems under in the name of so and so."

When one starts writing then it's all imagination. I had a portable fireplace carried to the verandah. It was raining. I burnt all my writings, and I cried and cried.

Everything that I wrote, I burnt. I told my wife, "Since you don't like me being a poet. Here it is." I took a vow not to write anything again. "The poet in me is dead. I won't write."

Then I came here to Surrey, where I am a member of the Indo-Canadian Senior Society. The last Sunday of every month we have a poetry session for two hours. We're all seniors, many of them write themselves, and some of them read or recite somebody else's poem. I joined them in 2012. I used to go there and listen to them.

I realized that I could write better than many of them. So I started writing poems again. It was a sort of rebirth of a poet: a resurrection, a second chance. I wrote poems competitively. The quality of my poems was commended by the audience and applauded.

Around January 2015, almost a year and a half ago, I realized that it was not the end of life. I don't want to be honoured or to be praised by others. Life is not that small. Since I have my own other ways of life. Life is better and fuller than what it was. If I don't write it and people say, "Why don't you write it?"

I say, "I don't want to force myself to write a poem. The moment it comes, I write."

6. *Kartar Singh Meet – Standing for What is Right*

I was a student of grade 5 and I had joined the High School. The Mathematics paper consisted of 12 questions and the option was to do any 10 questions. I finished my entire mathematic paper consisting of all 12 questions in less than half the time allotted. I wrote a note on top that could amount to a challenge to the teacher. I said, "Check any 10 questions."

It was a big challenge.

And when the results came, the teacher gave me 48 out of 50 marks and gave 50 out of 50 to another student. When the results were shown to us, I stood up in the class and questioned the teacher.

I said, "Why have you given me 48 marks and 50 to him?"

He couldn't justify it.

Ultimately I blurted out, "You gave him 50 marks only because he's from your village and you're neighbours." And the teacher slapped me but I never regretted it because I had the courage to challenge the teacher for what I thought was right.

7. *Bernadette Law – My Adopted Brother*

My mother and father had 5 daughters, and my grandmother wanted my father to get a second and even a third wife until he got a baby boy to carry the family name.

It was during the wartime, and many men went to fight for the country and many men died on the battlefield. Many wives and children were back in the street with no food.

One night there was a beggar woman came with a few children and she said, "My baby is only a few months old. I can't leave the baby with the children, because they are all under 9 years old. If you take my baby, I can go an work and the rest of the children will have something to eat."

So she handed the baby to my mother, and put it in her arms. My mother looked at the baby, and found that the baby was cute. And while she was playing with the baby, the beggar left with her children.

What could my mother do? She brought it home, inside the house, and found out that it was a boy. Now we had a boy to carry the family name, so we don't have to worry about my father getting a second or third wife. So my mother and father had to look after so many children and it was very difficult for them.

We still lived in the same place, and the baby's mother might pop by and just have a look, and that's all. But she wasn't able to support all the children, so she didn't want the baby back.

We had difficulty with the adopted boy because people told him that he was adopted so your parents aren't good to you.

We studied very hard, but he didn't study hard, because people told him, "You study hard and you work, and make money, all the money will go to the family, not to you." He thought that was true.

But I don't think he had the talent to study like other people. So he didn't study well in school. One time when he was about 14 years old, he thought, "I'd better go back to my own family." So he went there for about two weeks, and found that things were not so great. He came back to us.

Actually we treated him very well, because he was the only boy. My father always had his picture taken with my oldest sister and my younger brother, but not the ones in between. Usually the parents like the first one, and then when you have the second and third, it's not that interesting, but when you've got a boy, then it's different. So he'd dress up like a soldier, or whatever, for the pictures with my father.

He quit school and he got a job, but not a very good job. I paid for him to go to evening classes. I went there to the class, and he didn't show up. And I paid with my own money to get him to study.

Later my brother-in-law took him into his company, and he worked there until he died. So he had a productive life. He had one boy and one girl. That was really good for him, to have one of each. But his children didn't study either. They ended up doing trades, like carpentry. The girl got a friend from the internet. They didn't do that well.

His wife left him when the children were young. Later on, she would come for a visit, and the children would say, "Mother's coming. Hide everything valuable."

But he was good to my parents later.

8.   Bernadette Law – Bound Feet.

I don't know, starting when? Someone, a concubine she liked small feet. She thought that everyone should have small feet, just like here, people have high-heeled shoes, and they think that when you have high-heeled shoes, the way you stand and the way you walk is so elegant. With small feet you do the same thing, and you carry a handkerchief, and you wave it just so, and they think that is a kind of beauty. You walk straight because of the bound feet.

Only rich people could do that. If you are poor, you can't, because you have to work. If you have a little bit of money in the family, the children, the girls, got their feet bound.

It's very, very painful. As you're growing and your feet get longer and bigger, but every day you have to bind them so they won't spread. For beauty. That shows that your family has some money, and you're wealthy, and you can afford to do that. Someone who works in the field or is a servant can't do that.

When they went out, the servants carried them on their backs. The girls were not supposed to go out. They didn't go to school, because they should be staying at home and doing embroidery.

I don't know why they think it's beauty, because I look at the feet and they're so ugly to me.

My grandmother had bound feet. She was born about 1880. Her family was well off, so she had her feet bound. She married and her husband died at about 30 years old, and she was widowed with one son. She did sewing to make a living. The Law family, in the family, there are so many brothers and sisters and so on. Every so often, when there is a festival, there is food and the jobs are divided to different families, so she managed to survive. My father had a few years of education.

She could write beautiful calligraphy. During the Chinese New Year she made all the blessings and "may your wish come true" and all those kind of things.

She moved to Hong Kong and brought the whole family. My grandmother was always the highest in the family. We all respect people who are older and in a superior situation. All she did at home was maybe help a little bit with cutting the vegetables. She just did things like that. But she was good at sewing. She could sit very straight without a chair back, and none of us could do that.

But she just sat.

And our seniors, when we did something, they didn't have to say, "Thank you." Just, "Pick this up," and you pick it up. No "Thank you." This was the way.

She did sewing, and if she said, "Oh, I dropped a needle," then you had to pick it up for her.

9.   *Graham Mallet – Life in The Risk*

When I was five we moved to a little settlement called The Risk. There was a two-room school there. My father taught at that.

It was a dairy farming area, so all the people around us had farms. We had a couple of our own cows, house cows, for our own milk.

We didn't have any electricity. We got electricity when I was 15. We didn't have a phone until after the war. I was 8 when we got a phone. And our phone number was 7. The telephone exchange was in the post office. In Australia the telephones were all owned by the Post Office. It was a farmhouse about a quarter of a mile from where we lived. It was the telephone exchange and it was there we got our mail, too.

So before we got our phone, if either of my parents were wanted on the phone, the lady that ran the telephone exchange would come out and ring a cow bell, and they would run up the hill and take the phone call.

If you wanted a particular number you just rang, left the handset on and rang the phone around once, then picked up the telephone and the lady at the exchange picked it up.

My best friend's parents' number was 9. So I remember if I wanted to speak to him I couldn't say, "Will you give me number 9?" because that would be considered too formal and she would be insulted. So I would have to ask for someone by name.

"I'd like to speak to Bruce Wilson, please."

"Okay, that's fine."

But most of the time I was still a bit scared of the phone, and he lived about a mile away, and if I wanted to talk to my friend I'd walk because the phone was a bit too scary for me.

So after I finished elementary school I commuted on a school bus. It was kind of a general passenger bus, and all the school kids went on it to the nearest high school, which was 13 miles away on Granville road, a place called Kyogle. I went to high school there. There were 12 in my graduating class. 6 boys and 6 girls, so we had great times. We got along well, but it was a very small arrangement.

When we went away for university, again, it was a little country town, a small university that had just opened and there were 250 students total at that time. So they all knew us by name.

10.   *Sandy Long – Iranian Electrical Systems*

We lived and worked in Iran and we were stationed in a recreational subdivision about a kilometre inland from the Caspian coast. It was relatively new cottages that were erected for vacation people from Tehran in the summer, but we lived there year round. They were fairly modern and well constructed superficially. However, some of their electrical – it was 1975 – wasn't up to any code that I can imagine because part way through our stay, there were several things happen that made us suspect the electricity.

Number one, I think a dog was electrocuted in the swamp across the street from our house, and there were dead frogs all over the place. We had an Asian toilet in our entryway, and it had a cistern up high like the British system, and that's where the flush water was stored, with a loo chain with a pull knob on it that came down from the tank, so you could flush this tank that was up well above my head height, up near the ceiling.

One particular stormy night we heard some crackling in the Asian bathroom area and looked in there to see the loo chain was glowing yellow, red, hot, and also the electrical meter was running backwards at a rapid rate. We knew there was something wrong with the electricity.

I did at one time look up into the attic through the crawl space. It was just a birdsnest of wires, heading in every direction across the rafters. They were just twisted together. There were no marettes, no proper joins or junction boxes, they just got up there and twisted them all together. It was darned lucky we didn't burn down.

I assume the sewer was a good ground, and the house was poorly grounded, and somehow there was some object leaning against the plumbing and there must have been a hot wire touching somewhere. And of course it was 220 volt.

11.   Jen Melville-Roberts – Life in England

I was born in 1930 in Sealchart, which is just outside of Sevenoaks, just outside London. There were three of us: Pam, myself, and Rosemary. I'm the middle one.

Our father died when I was 4 and Rosemary was 9 months old. Mother moved to Pinner. I don't remember anything about there, then Ruyslip, which I remember. It was on the outskirts of London, and it was almost countryside, then.

He was in his early forties when they got married. I know our mother was in her late thirties.

Then we were living in London just before WW II definitely, because we went to a private school that our mother had gone to, in Penzance, out in Cornwall.

I remember going to kindergarten because we always had to learn an instrument, and I can remember learning the triangle. That was in Ruyslip. I must have been 7 when I went away to school.

We had family in Cornwall, so it wasn't a hardship to go away to boarding school, because we saw them every weekend. The family was always there. Our mother was born in Penzance. All three of us went to school there together.

Then Pam went to the Welsh Girls' School, which was in Ashford, just outside London. It was a school that was set up for the children of Welsh parents living in England. Our father was Welsh. That was his connection with Lloyd George. Our grandfather was obviously very comfortably off. We know that he was involved with a lot of community things, because he was a barrister. Our father ended up being a merchant in the City of London. I think, but I'm not sure, that it's tied up with the Masonic Lodge. I got a grant to go to school from one of the merchant companies. This was not uncommon in England if you knew the ropes. But our father may have started when he came over to Canada, because he had a fur and leather importing business.

It's interesting, because on Pam's birth certificate, it has "of independent means." On my birth certificate, two years later, it has "merchant in the City of London."

He obviously didn't have any money, because my grandfather had all his money embezzled by his partner.

We were living in London at the early part of the war, but our house got bombed. But fortunately I had a godfather who had been like a father to us. They had a very large house in Pinner, where we had lived as children, with a three-acre garden and a full-time gardener.

He started off with nothing. He started off as an office boy with a paper company in London, and he did very well.

When we were bombed, we went to live with him, because their family had left home. They had two boys in the army and I think Hill was still at school, then. We lived there all through the war. I had to stop going to school in Penzance, because all the costal towns were barred, because it was a seaside resort, and the Germans could have got in there easily.

So then I went to – they had these schools in England, I don't know how my mother heard about this. They were called the Parent's National Education Union Schools. They weren't Union. They were actually all private schools. I went to one until I was 13, and then I moved to one that just had more senior girls, in Shropshire, in Ludlow. Mother didn't want Pam and I at the same school because we were so close to one another in age that she thought we would be better at separate schools.

It didn't worry me at all. I think boarding school makes you independent. I guess in a way mother had to be very independent. It was tough on her. Our father was obviously very comfortably off, but then of course the 1930s were a bad time, and then father dying, I guess any money that they had soon went.

Mother had worked before she got married; she worked in a bank. She worked for a company that made toothpaste. She was with them for a long time. But our mother had led a really sheltered life. Her elder half-brother was 27 or 28 when she was born. I can remember her saying that when she went to school, she was never allowed to go on her own, and if it was wet, I think either a car or a carriage took her to school.

Young girls like that, I don't know whether we actually walked to school on our own. It wasn't very far, especially when we lived in Ruyslip. I guess we did lead sheltered lives. But we weren't spoiled. Mother never had the money to pamper us anyway. Looking back on it, we have often thought that it was absolutely amazing. Our mother took us to art galleries, took us to museums. Every fall before we went back to school she would say, "Do you want to go to the theatre or the ballet?" She used to go to the ballet with us. It was amazing.

And I guess to a certain extent she did it because her father was an artist, her elder brother was an artist who ran one of the London Schools of Art. This is where I came by my interest in the Arts.

The only thing, I don't know if Mother liked Opera. I don't remember ever going to opera. We went to plays and that.

12. *Mohammed Abadula – Walking to Pakistan*

My name is Mohammed and today I will be sharing a story from the year of 1947. That was the time when Pakistan and India were separating. They used to be under British influence, but the British were not interested in that area any more and they planned to leave. So the Muslim community there decided that they would make their own country.

So one night my great-great-grandparents and my great-grandparents tried to sneak out of the country. My grandfather was one and one half years old at that time.

Around sundown they started, travelling through the wheat fields. My grandfather was crying and shouting, and people in the group even suggested leaving him. But my great-grandmother was stubborn and calmed him down in the end.

At about dawn they found a truck that was going to Pakistan. So instead of walking there, they decided to hitch a ride. Once they got there, since they were sneaking out of the country, they had nothing. No property, no money.

In time the government gave my family some land they could farm, and I've actually been to that farm. It's in a small community. And that's the story of how my family came from India to Pakistan and settled there.

13.   Sue Murguly – Hungarian Education

This is really funny. My sister refused to go to Kindergarten unless she could take me with her. So I went to Kindergarten early. I was in Kindergarten for two years, while my sister went on to Grade 1. So basically I was three years old when I started. In Hungary there was Junior and Senior Kindergarten. I think because I started early I could skip the second year and go into Grade 1. I don't know how that happened. My sister and I both started Grade 1 when we were 7 years old, because September 1 was the cutoff date, and we were born in September and we just missed the cutoff day, and we had to wait another year.

The school was a two-or three-storey brick building with stucco on the outside. The rooms were big. There were about 25 kids in a class. One teacher, and she taught everything. It was somewhat political. I still remember reading this story about this girl who went and coloured the leaves with blue pencil, and the teacher went up and said, "Why did you colour the leaves blue?" and she said, "I don't have a green pencil."

Then the teacher went – this is the socialist idea – "How come you did not share your green pencil with the person who didn't have one?" It was a lesson in sharing.

We had a gymnasium in the school and we had a wonderful playing field. I remember when you were doing the high jump, and you had to clear a certain height, and that was one thing I had a problem with. I saw that stupid bar across there, and it scared the heck out of me. Anyway, they worked with me until I could clear it, because that was really important.

I thought the school system was run well. I remember my sister having problems reading, and the teacher coming to my Mum saying, "She needs to learn how to read this by this time," and it was up to my mother to deal with this.

There were no children left behind because you worked until you got up to a certain level. I loved it, because I did well.

Their method of teaching was to call you up to the board to demonstrate your knowledge. A lot of board work, just a few students at a time would come up. Geography was the same way. You had to memorize and you had to be able to point where the places were on the map. It was interactive in this sense.

Hungarian is not a difficult language to read because it's phonetic. The way you write it is the way you pronounce it. So as soon as you knew the Hungarian alphabet you would be able to tie the letters together to read. But they did a lot through recitation. Reciting poetry, reciting passages, and we started that in Grade 1. You had long poems to recite in Grade 1, I remember. I only went to that school in Grade 1, Grade 2, and till Christmas in Grade 3, when we left.

I remember a lot of, it wasn't real gymnastics, it was mainly working with ropes and hoops and drills like rhythmic gymnastics moves, with everybody moving together with music playing. I remember hoops. We would put a ribbon around it to make it colourful. Weird things you remember, as a child.

And Art. I remember having to draw this kid. Now whether I was in Grade 2 or Grade 1, and I can't remember, and I had to draw this kid on a bike with a pencil. They had an example of it, and you practice until you have everything right. Then you could move on to the next project. A lot of repetition. Your grades ran from 1 to 5, with 5 being the best, and there were awards at the end of the year if you got straight 5s. That was a big deal.

14. Benjamin and Evita – Problems with the World

The problem started when we had children. When my children were born and they were growing up I was thinking that they needed to learn English. I put my children to study English in Mexico. But it was not possible to learn to speak good English in Mexico. Then I met a family who lived in Canada. So I worked hard to send my children to live in Canada. We went to visit the Canadian Embassy in Mexico City. Then Canada opened the doors to my children so they could come here. They were 15, 12, and 18 years old.

The family that lived in Canada was from El Salvador. Through them, we had a place where people can bring their children to Canada, and the Embassy gave us permission for my children to live with this family in Canada.

Miriam was 18 years old when she went to Canada. Samai was 15 years old, and Obed was 12 years. We sent them one by one. The first visit was for two years each. After that, they liked Canada, and they applied to come to Canada for good.

My wife was very sad when the children were in Canada, but we knew that we were doing the best thing for them.

15.   Benjamin – Land Grab

In the beginning all the land in Mexico was owned by the government. But after the Revolution, that land was given out to the people of Mexico. My grandfather got about 8 different pieces of land, so many kilometers of area, and he gave it to my father.

We came here to Canada to visit our children when they became permanent residents. When we were here in Canada, some other Mexican people thought that I would not come back to Mexico. This was my first big problem. When I came back to Mexico again after five years, the government of Mexico told me, "You are not the owner of anything. Go back to Canada."

"Where is my land? It came from my father. I didn't buy it. It is the heritage of my father." The government Heritage Department investigated and found that the other people could take the property. They asked that person, "How did you become the owner of that land? Why are you working this land?"

"Because they left for another country."

"But who authorized you to take this land?"

Then the conflict became between the lawyers for each person. But they had a meeting with the local Government Land Representative who was the authority in general. And he defended the other people who became the owners of the land.

And they all got together as a group and I returned to Canada without anything.

But the next year my friends sent me a message that the local Land Representative had died. The new Representative knew my story, and he said, "I know the whole story. The whole town knows that land is owned by the teacher, Benjamin."

Then they had a new hearing, and called the people together. I was in Mexico at that time, and they asked the others how they became owners of this land. And their defence was that I had abandoned the land and did not work the land. That was the reason. Nobody knows who abandoned the land without working it.

When I gave my side, I told them that I didn't stop working the land. I paid for people to grow beans and corn. Even if I didn't stay in Mexico the land was giving fruit. "Come and see." I said.

But the most important part of it was that I did not buy the land. I inherited it from my father. This is the under the authorities that knew my father. And this is the reason, according to the law, the heritage cannot be changed for somebody else.

At this time everybody stood, and the representative of the government said, "It is clear that Professor Benjamin is the owner of the land." And at that time I became owner of the land in Mexico again. And then I needed to sleep beside my wife, because I was exhausted.

Now I only have the memories of that land. Some of it, I gave it away to my children. The rest of it, I sold to finance coming to Canada and to buy here and live here. And with that money we even bought a burial plot. Everything.

And now with that money I still pay my friends. I have no problems with money.

I always had documents that I owned the land. But these people stole the land and pretended that the land was from somebody else. But because I got the papers to say that I was the owner, and the original owner was my father's father.

I had the original papers with all the signatures, but the other person who became the second owner only had signatures from the local office, not the federal government. And the judge said, "These are not true. The original papers are true."

The other people lied and bribed the local officials to make documents, but they only had local signatures. The magistrate gave the land to the others because they bribed him. It was corruption.

3.   Life in Canada

1.   *Anne Williams – Growing up in Canada.*

I was born in the Netherlands. I came with the family when I was about 3 years old. We went to Winnipeg, Manitoba because there were other family people there. My father was a farmer. I was brought up on a farm. It was for cows, a cow farm. We had the cows and other small animals: ducks and geese and chickens and so on.

We went to school just outside of Winnipeg, Dunak School. I only had grade 8 education. It was just about a 15-minute walk from our home. I was lucky. It was just a small school. 8 grades in 1 room and one teacher. So the education was kinda scant.

Then I went as a clerk and a waitress. I worked in a laundry for a while, in the linen room of St. Paul's Hospital. It was good. Just filling big carts of linen for the different floors of the hospital. By then I had a little room of my own in town. I went to work there.

I was a waitress and he came in and ordered his meal. I gave him his meal. He ate the whole thing from start to finish, even the desert. And then he wanted the whole thing repeated. We were so astonished that the boss said, "Just charge him for one."

So I thought, "A man with that kind of humour would be pretty good."

And he kept hanging around after he met me, and we eventually got married. He was an airline pilot, and we had four children. I stayed in Winnipeg. It was a pretty good life. I had a wonderful husband. He died though, too early. He was only 63 when he died. By this time we had moved to British Columbia a year.

2.   *Cal Whitehead - More school Stories*

I don't remember much more about Grade 1 than I've already told, Grade 2. But Grade 3 was something else for me. That's when we learned how to write with pen and ink. And I was left handed, and my mother had told that school, under no circumstances was he to be turned into a right-handed person. The pen nib kept digging into the cheap paper and splattering all over the place. I splattered all over. The teacher kept pouring more ink into my inkwell, and I would go home covered with ink and scrub it off. I learned how to print more than write. That was Grade 3.

Grade 4 I had, in retrospect, a very important time. I didn't know it at the time. I loved to read. I read everything. And one day we had a very special exam. Mrs. Bold gave us a little booklet. "This is an examination."

And I struggled on, and I struggled on and I finished the book, and I was so disappointed that I had finished the book. She gave a second one, and it was more difficult than the first, and I was right in the middle of that book when the bell rang, and I had to hand it in. I didn't attach any importance to this, but the next year in Grade 5, there was a woman called in from retirement because of the death of the Grade 5 teacher, and she was quite overweight and quite elderly, and it was fascinating watching her dentures shift.

She wore this naked green dress all the time, hanging down unevenly around her shins. And she said, "You know, if you make special effort this year you can skip Grade 6 and go into Grade 7."

Well, I forgot all about that, and I just made my own achievement. I covered the phases of the moon and the tides in Vancouver, and the shipping, particularly two Dutch-American ships called Oranji and something else, and I tracked them in their journeys down to Hawaii, Fiji, New Zealand and Australia. And they'd radio back, and I'd know from the tiny little slivers in the Shipping News where they were and what they were doing.

I even got a glimpse of the Oranji where it was docked, 12,000 tons, very rusty and mismatched painting. One day it was docked right beside an Empress boat. Pristine white. Everything was white. And I said, "I love my ship anyway."

And at the end of it I got into Grade 7. Small for my age, wearing short pants in Grade 7, and four of the boys were over 6 feet. Elmo Trasollini was the chief among them. He was a celebrity, because his brother was the pitcher of the Vancouver semi-pro baseball. He and his three buddies would bully the younger and smaller boys, but not me. I had all the answers to all the questions, and I could slip them the answers. So I knocked off the bullying.

The teacher in Grade 7 was only about 18 years old, fresh out of Normal School.

One day after recess there was this funny smell in the room. And Miss Newcome said, "Who's been eating garlic?"

Elmo and his buddies stood up like heroes, you know.

Miss Newcome fell into tears, and the girls all got around her and hugged her and chewed out those boys with words that hadn't been in the syllabus. Oh, and the boys expected to be honoured, but boy, they were chewed out very well.

There were two twins; their name was Bauder. Dave and Alvin. And Alvin and I hit it off very nicely, especially in the math part. I later ran into them at university, and Dave was a mechanical engineer and Alvin was in engineering physicist, the top level. And we still got along very well, but we didn't see very much of each other. He was at university, and I was engaged every minute of every day in extracurricular activities and hovering around the failing mark in my curricular work.

3.   Cal Whitehead – Flatness

There is the story of a Saskatchewan farmer who goes out in his field and he looks to the west, and if he gets up on his tiptoes, he can see the back of his neck.

The farmer visited the west, and his grandchild said, "What did you think of the West?"

He said, "Well, it'd be fine if they moved them darned mountains."

4.   Cal Whitehead – John Fisher

Further to my schooling at Florence Nightingale School in Vancouver.

I entered Grade 1 being introduced by my older sister. She was really my teacher since she was starting Grade 3, she had taught me the first two grades before I got to the first. So I was there and very early in the year the teacher said, "Now busy yourself with plasticene or something while Mr. Fisher gets his equipment all ready."

And there was this young man there who was setting up a projector, 16 mm film and spools and lighting and whatnot. I pieced it together later that that Mr. Fisher was John Fisher who became very famous. He was only a teenager in 1932 and that's when I saw him. He showed films from coast to coast to coast, and that was my first hearing of that particular phrase. And I have done that, coast to coast to coast. So he showed pictures of the Arctic, particularly Tuktoyaktuk, a name that stokes my memory.

When I got home for lunch that day, I said, "Mom, can I go to Tuktoyaktuk?"

She said, "Well, not right now, son, but keep it in your mind, and one day you're sure to get there, and sure enough 68 years later, I did. We drove up a few years ago the Dempster Highway. Dempster was a very prominent Mountie a hundred years before. We flew on because the roads were too soft. We flew into Tuktoyaktuk, and the chief's daughter showed us around. Her English was excellent, normal English. She had been educated in Calgary. She showed us her father's dog team, off for the summer. Fierce, fierce dogs, and each one on a short chain and sitting on a laced wood framework so the droppings would go right through. She said, "We water them twice a week, and we feed them once a week. They get a whole raw fish. Frozen."

A young Chinese fellow, one of nine in the group, put his hand out, and the dog snapped at it, and he raised it just in time. And he lowered it again, the dog snapped at it. This went on for three times. Finally the dog got tired of it and allowed himself to be petted.

That was more in modern times, but I heard about it from John Fisher. And he said, "I tell you kids, see and know Canada first."

And when I met Faye, she said, "Oh, I love Mexico."

And I said, "Okay, but we've got to see Canada first."

We went to the end of this highway, and the end of that highway, and to this big lake and that small city, and we did the whole thing, coast to coast to coast, stayed with friends in Newfoundland and saw off the coast the island where the birds are. I forget. Where the puffins are. And we saw them in their activities.

So sure enough, my mother was right.

5.   *Fay Whitehead – John Fischer*

This is really Cal's story but I'm telling it. John Fischer was a man who was known as Mr. Canada because he talked about Canada, telling Canada, telling stories about Canada, mostly to school children, but he also had a 15-minute radio program. He happened to be giving a talk to Cal's class, his grade 1 class, when Cal was 6, and he told stories including Tuktoyaktuk. When he finished his little talk with the children with the advice to the children that they should see and know Canada first. Travel is great, see the world, but see Canada first.

So when I was trying to get Cal to go to Mexico, which was the country I had fallen in love with in Grade 5, no, we couldn't go there because we hadn't seen enough of Canada first.

Anyway, Cal went home from school that day and asked his mother if he could go to Tuktoyaktuk. His mother stopped and thought and said, "You just keep that in your mind, and one of these days you'll get there."

Well, he did finally. 11 years ago, in 2005, we took a driving trip up through British Columbia and into the Yukon and Northwest Territories. We drove partway on the Alcan Highway, and we drove the Dempster Highway to Inuvik, and then we flew from Inuvik to Tuktoyaktuk, so he made it and he has a certificate to prove that he dunked his foot in the Arctic Ocean in amongst the ice that was floating. It was very brave

Also on that trip we went to Nahanni, which is where I wanted to go. We drove to Fort Simpson, and then flew and had three different stops and Nahanni, but we flew over the falls, Virginia Falls. There happened to be a rainbow over the falls when we were flying towards it, and we didn't catch that rainbow on the camera, but I'll never forget it.

We landed in this sort of curved area at the top of the falls, and we got out of the small bush plane, a Cessna, and walked, there's a board walk because the ground is muskeg and it's spongy, like walking on a mattress. So we walked on this boardwalk to the top of the falls and the water was getting rougher and rougher until it was really plunging, you know, and then went over the edge of the falls. It was quite thunderous. We were sitting on a bench, and we had some food with us. I brought out a banana each, and Cal said,

"Well, what's your impression?"

I said, "I will never forget watching the rapids going to the falls while sitting on a bench eating a banana."

6.   Fay Whitehead – Music

In Grade 5, I was 10 years old, a very impressionable age, and my teacher was Miss Oldfield, and she was a classical music buff. She would bring recordings of classical music, and another class would be invited to come and join us and we'd team up in these little desks and little seats, bench seats, you know, and she would play us classical music, and she would explain it, she would explain the story behind the music, what it represented, and the instruments that were used, and the solo instruments she would point out what they were, and I became very conscious of music. I had taken piano lessons for five years, and my mother had wanted piano lessons and never got them, so I was the privileged one, only I didn't feel that way about it. I wanted to sing to music, or I wanted to dance to music. I didn't want to play piano. And I hated every minute of it.

And finally one day I got up enough nerve to save mum the 50 cents for the teacher because I just didn't want to go.

But I kept my love of music, and I still love to dance, I can still cha-cha-cha and I'm 83, but I met a woman that I was friends with who was a jazz enthusiast, and she taught me how to listen to jazz. It's best if you close your eyes. You can hear much better if you close your eyes.

She was a pianist, trained as a concert pianist, but she was so shy she would get stage fright and she would not be able to perform, to the great disappointment of her parents.

This was in Toronto, and we would go together to the visiting jazz specialists from the States mostly, and she would want to sit in a place where she could watch the hands on the piano.

She could not play jazz. She was trained in Classical, but she was not able to switch over. It was too big a jump, and she couldn't play it, but she enjoyed it, so we would go and see Dave Brubeck and Duke Ellington. We were so close to Duke Ellington that he kept his glass of lemon coffee – he did not drink alcohol. Coffee with lemon on it – he would have that on the table just behind him, and that was our table. We would be that close to watch him play. So I also kept my love of jazz. We love to listen to CBC jazz in the evenings.

7. Fay Whitehead – Back to the Land

My maiden name was duBois. My father came from Northern Ireland, so we're Huguenot descendants. Dad came to Canada when he was 16. I never did ask him why. He was the oldest boy in the family and why would he leave the family? I'm curious about that now, and now it's too late to ask.

He worked on a wheat farm in Saskatchewan and then he joined the Canadian Army in the First World War, and when he returned he got off the train at Toronto and subsequently met my mother, who was born in Steiner Ontario, near Collingwood. She had come down to Toronto to get away from the farm, I think.

They married, and I'm the baby of three children. Quite the baby. In other words, my brother was 10 ½ years older and my sister was 8 years older than I was, so I was almost an only child.

We lived in the Bathhurst-St. Claire area; in fact we lived on the same street as Casa Loma for nine years. Our backyard fence was the school fence, so I gained very bad habits in that I could be finishing my breakfast when the school bell would ring, and I would not be late for school. But it caused me to have bad habits. I was always late for work. I had very understanding bosses, though.

I worked in an office for 16 years, and then decided that I didn't really like that at all, and quit. I met a group of artist friends and I had learned to spin and weave. I was very interested in pioneer living, and then I met a friend who was making silk scarves with batik, that's hot wax and dyes, and they layer, so two colours could give you three colours, and then a third colour could give you five colours. So we did scarves and squares and dress lengths and we also did hangings, so that was a little more artistic than just the scarves.

So I did that for eight years and then in the meanwhile Cal and I had got married, and he said to me, "What kind of house do you want?"

And I said, "First choice, log, second choice, stone."

He found me a log house. With no plumbing. An hour from Toronto, half an hour from Hamilton. We lived there for 20 years and loved every minute of it. I left my batik work after 10 years and Cal was not ready to make any major change. He was quite happy with what he was doing.

So I said, "Well, we are sitting on 11 acres, why don't we do something on them?"

We had some Dutch neighbors, very involved in growing things. We asked Bill his advice as to how we could start making some use of our land, and he suggested a beehive. So we spent the winter tap-tap-tapping, building our beehive. We went on from there with chickens, ducks, geese, turkeys, and goats, making use of all the produce that we had. We also had to have a kitchen garden and then eventually a larger field garden to feed the animals in the wintertime.

The first winter with the goats we were scrounging at local produce stores to get the outer leaves of cabbage and lettuce and things like that and buying a 50 lb. bag of carrots to feed them. Eventually we got our own garden. We had a small field, probably only an acre, where we grew some hay, but we had to buy the hay for the goats.

We did that for another 10 years, and then one night I said to Cal, "Can you picture us living here in this house in our old age?"

And he said, "No,"

So we sat and made up an ad for the Toronto Star and put it in, and nothing happened. We did have a few calls. We had a few people come and look. We put it in for a second week, and then it was a good week after that we finally got a phone call.

This young woman came out, she and her mother. "Oh! You can live in this log house!"

We had said it was a historic log house, a pioneer house. It was a good 150 years old.

She and her sister bought it and they lived there for 14 years. We moved on to a bigger farmhouse east of Toronto, north of Colburg, and we lived there for 14 years, and then we had been talking about moving to B. C. and I said to Cal, "It would be a terrible shame if we move out to BC after your mother dies.

So we got out there in time to spend two years with her. She almost reached 96. So we spent a lot of time with her, making up for the two brothers who had been looking after her pretty well full time.

Cal's sister had already died, and his father. But we spent some good time with Mum, and so here we are, in Surrey, B. C.

8.   *Joan Campbell – My Life*

My brother, he's 93. There's longevity in our DNA, but lots of tragic losses through war, for the men, you know. My older brother, the doctor, he was killed in an accident. Accidents are awful things. My younger brother is still alive. My brother's wife had to talk to him often. He was way too protective of me. Thought he should tell me what to do. Then the next day he would suddenly say – I know it was his wife that talked to him – he would say, "I realize that you've been on your own in a totally new country and you've managed your own life."

I became myself, you know. Emotionally and physically grown up. Because I had studied physio. I thank my mother. She wanted me to be a nurse, but I got burnt as a probationer, badly burnt in a steamer accident, and I had to drop out. Given time to think about it, I chose physio, because it was the nearest thing to being a nurse, and I never regretted it, never regretted it, because it came into its own. Then it became a highly qualified profession. In Montreal, McGill has wonderful training, and UBC was great.

I have worked in Canada, in America, in Germany, in South Africa, and England. But always part time. Because with children. I always took time off for the children. I was meant to have children. Having children was very important. I had good pregnancies. I always enjoyed being pregnant. Until the end. Which wasn't so good, but I enjoyed being pregnant. So I had three girls.

My life, my experience of living, and we live in such a difficult world, but an exciting world in many ways. So I am grateful every day for the rest of my life.

Someone said to me, "Joan, I want you to invite me to your 100th birthday." I said, "Oh, please!"

But I look back on my upbringing, and go right through I think all children want to run against each other and compete, to wrestle; I could wrestle my eldest brother to the ground when I was about 11, and then my mother took me aside and said, "No more wrestling." Because I adored my mother, my life changed. But all children want to be free to climb trees and wrestle with each other, but have a secure love of the family.

And the moment we stepped into the house we had discipline and we knew how we had to behave. But outside we would run wild, and throw bad apples, hiding in the trees, you know, at people we didn't like. We did naughty things. All children do naughty things. Wonderful life. I've had a wonderful life.

9.   Darryl Catton – Music

I was working in the steam plant and when I got out of there for a while I thought I'd join the station band. So I went over and they have a room off base a little bit. And the guy that ran the band, the bandmaster, he hated officers. He had no respect for any of them. He was a flight sergeant, that's three stripes and a crown, and he was just retiring.

I used to like the band. You'd go up there and loosen your tie. I was trying to get out of the CEO's parade, too. They have the CEO's parade. When you're working in the steam plant, you're not in uniform because you can't be. Going in the CEO's parade you gotta go home and change and clean up and shine your shoes, and I got tired of that, so I thought I'd get out of it by going into this band. Then I found out they were the station band, so they had to attend every function. So this one function the Sergeant, his name was Craybourne, he was retiring, so he was going to put on a show. We went to wait on the tarmac for the dignitary. I think he was something in West Germany, the defense minister or something. And it was hot. You know in the service when you're out on the tarmac waiting for some dignitary, you got an open file, and you gotta stand there rigidly at attention and it gets pretty hot, and some of the dignitaries they don't want to go through this either. They want to get over to the officer's mess and get a drink.

We had numbers on our music. So down the guy comes, and the commanding officer, and there's a senior warrant officer, he's the guy who's the disciplinary. If there's anybody out of line he'll write a line down on your form. There's several people in line. So they come over and they do the troops, first row, second row, third row, but we always play them this piece of music, and it's like a Russian death march. Slow, so they walk on slow, So Crayborn, taps, "We're playing 76," or whatever it was. 76 Trombones. "What? We can't play that." Well, maybe he'll tone it down. No way, right in time. So what the heck. You can't play that. We played it. It was a brass band, too.

Well that dignitary went down the line and up the line, and down the line. After they do that, they always come over and talk to the band. I was right in the front, I was a one-valve trumpet player, and I was in the front so I heard every word. He came over and the commanding officer, his face was just red, because he was staunch military, and you just don't do that, and he was ready to give Creebo hell, but this dignitary came over and shook his hand, "This is the best parade I've ever been on. I have to commend you." Of course he had a chest full of ribbons. They go over to the officer's mess for a beer. I guess he just wanted this formality to end.

Well, the CEO couldn't say nothin' then. So they disbursed except for the band. We had to go back to the band hall. Craybourne was pretty proud of himself. He was getting out the next day. So we all fell out behind him except one snare drum. And he's going up the street, and gets to the officer's mess, and they're all looking out the windows, and he timed it so that we'd be right there, and he brings down his baton and played this piece, and all you heard was "rat-a-tat- tat-tat" and one little beep. We're walking along the sidewalk. Took the wind right out of his sails.

10.   Joanne Harris – Steno Work in Montreal

In 1951 I travelled to Montreal and I had no trouble finding employment because I had worked in Winnipeg for five years. I had various living arrangements, always sharing with other girls. This was for economy reasons. I played golf in the summer time, I skied in the winter time, and I had a good time.

But my brother who was there went to the US. There were better opportunities for him when he graduated from McGill.

So one Saturday night I picked up the newspaper and there were statistics there saying there were 40,000 more women than men in Montreal. So I decided to go west. I resigned from TCA, and I travelled to Vancouver by train, with all my belongings and I joined Office Overload. I was shopping for employment. I didn't know where the best places would be to work, but I knew that a forest products company would be okay.

Working for Office Overload kind of backfired because in some places I stayed so long that it defeated the purpose, and also when I was opening the mail in one place and I saw the bill for my services, and I thought, "This is no good. They're making more money than I am."

So I quit. I joined McMillian Blodel, where I stayed for six years.

On New Year's Eve of 1965/66 I went to a house party. My cousin had invited me, and I said, "I don't want to be number three or number five at a New Year's Eve party, so I'll babysit for you."

She said that there were going to be two spares there. So that swung the needle. I said, "I will come."

I arrive at this party and I'm looking for these two spares, and one was three sheets to the wind. He didn't have a hope in heck. The other one was sitting in a corner. Butter wouldn't melt in his mouth. He might as well have been reading a book. But he was the winner. We were engaged February 28, married April 7, bought a house in August, moved in October 1, and we were there for forty-five years. Kadota drive.

11.   *Kendra Wilson – The Tube Ride*

My family was going to our cabin and we had some friends up there named Katie and Tanner. One day we were going to go for a tube ride, so I got up, got dressed, got ready to go, Everyone else got onto the boat, and I got onto the tube with Katie and my sister Jessica, and we started to go over a bunch of waves. It was so much fun until we got over to the wake, the area where a bunch of people that ride tubes normally tip.

We saw these huge waves after the boat had made a circle, and we went over them and we all flipped. First went Katie, second went me, and third went my sister, but she didn't fall off. She was still holding onto the tube, even when it was upside down, She was just getting dragged over the waves, bouncing up and down like a crazy lunatic. Then she decided, "Okay, I'm just going to let go. I can't do this anymore. I'm just going to let go."

Katie started to cry because she thought she was the only one that fell off. I cried, too, but I did hurt myself, getting a rope burn. Then like a minute later Tanner hopped in the water and we flipped the tube back over onto its proper side, hopped into the boat, and went back to shore.

12.   Joanne Harris – In the Grocery Store

I was planning to do some baking for a craft fair, so I went to Save-On foods to their bulk section to get supplies. I completed my shopping and I got into the express lane, and when I approached the cashier, she said to me, "Your groceries have been paid for."

I said, "What do you mean, 'They've been paid for'?"

She said, "The gentleman behind you has paid for your groceries."

So I turned to him, and I said, "You must be a millionaire."

He said, "No, my wife is."

I said, "Just a minute, I haven't finished shopping."

It was really unbelievable that somebody would pay for my groceries. They must have cost more than his did.

So with that I left, but as I went past, I said, "Hey, what day do you shop here?"

He said, "Thursdays."

I said, "Hey, that's good. I'll see you next Thursday."

13.   Deanna Vowles – Steak

I was going to Jenny Craig, always, all my life trying to lose weight. Anyway I had my two grandchildren with me, one was two, and one was three. And the three-year-old just seemed to have the brains, the whatever, the knowledge to come up with different things. And so we get out of the car, we cross the street, and we just about get to the door and I looked down and there are two beautiful steaks, wrapped up and raw, sitting on the sidewalk. And I said, "Oh my gosh, that must fallen out of someone's bag, it maybe got juicy or something and the bag got torn and the steaks fell out." I said, "Or maybe somebody was turning vegetarian or something and trying to make a statement." Then Devon looked at me and said, "Well grandma, it might be a steak-ment."

14.   Jack Lillico – Model T trip to Stetler

I can't remember the date that I went, but I could look it up in the book. We had a tour to Stetler and my son and I drove two Model Ts to Stetler, which is 60 miles east of Red Deer. It was a long trip.

When we arrived, there were 84 Model Ts from Texas, from Los Angeles, all up the coast, and from Canada. We were the only two guys that drove. We did a 2500 mile trip.

When we got there they scheduled a train trip which they put several cars on two flat railway cars and towed by a steam engine about two hours east of Stetler and back. That was an interesting trip.

On the way home we went into Red Deer and went up to Jasper and experienced the Icefields, but it was a long climb at about 5 miles an hour for these Model Ts to go up there. But it was an interesting trip, and we came back from Jasper down the Yellowhead to Kamloops and returned to Vancouver.

15.   Trace Johnston – Hair dye.

This was a couple of months ago, now, and I had wanted to get my hair dyed for quite a while, probably over a year. I decided I was going to do it, so my Mum got the dye. I put it in my hair, and I waited 20 or 30 minutes or however long it was suppose to be. I went in the shower to rinse it out. I rinsed it out and I looked in the washroom mirror, and it was orange.

I was, "Oh, no. That is not good."

And then I was like, "Okay, maybe we didn't put enough in." Because we only used a little bit. So we put more in, and then it turned it a lighter orange.

And I was like, "Aaarrrrgh!"

Then I was, "Oh, no, That is not good."

So I went to bed and then I had a dream about it. Then I woke up and I went, "Oh, yes, it was just a dream. Thank you. It was just a dream.

I went in the washroom to get ready, and I looked in the mirror, and, "Noooo! It was not a dream!" It was reality.

I was like, "That sucks!"

16.   Jack Lillico – Missing the Train

I was in Toronto, and decided to ride the rails back to Calgary, so the boys at the company I was at drove me down to the train and I checked my baggage on the train to the roomette, and they said, "we'd better go downstairs for a drink."

So about a quarter after 5, I heard a train rumbling out, and I looked at my ticket, and I thought it was 5:30, but it was 5:15. So I rushed up and got a cab and had the driver race to the west station of CPR and just as I got there the train was slowly pulling out, and one conductor was leaning on the door. If he hadn't been there I would have missed the train

He plonked the stairs down, and I went to my room, and all my baggage was on there, and there seemed to be nobody on that train for some reason.

But when I went down to the dining car I sat there and had my dinner, and there was a gentleman down the other side and I thought it was Crump of the railway, because they were looking after him really well. They were catering to him.

Finally he said, after dinner, "Come down and have a drink."

So I went to the table, and it was the cook there, and the steward, and various people and I didn't ever learn the guy's name until I got to the Lakehead, but anyway, we ran out of booze, and I said, "Well, I've got two bottles of Scotch in my room," which I brought. Finally the guy went to bed and the cook and I stayed up and polished off the other booze. I went down to bed, and I woke up in Blind River and I lifted the blind and here's this guy marching up the platform all pedukered up like he had a night's rest. I still didn't know his name.

Anyway, he marched out, and I said, "Oh, I don't want to see him this morning."

Well as soon as he got on the train, "Bang, bang," on the door, "Are you going to come down to the diner?"

So we went down to have breakfast, and I looked in the kitchen and the chef had his hat collapsed over and he was in rough shape.

We were in pretty good shape, because we were used to that.

Finally he got off the train at the Lakehead, and it was a janitorial company that he owned. Five trucks met him at the end of the rail and ushered him off to conduct his business. But I was sure it was Crump of the railway because they were treating him so well. But he was a big tipper, I guess.

That's the story of the train I almost missed.

(Ed. Note – Norris Roy "Buck" Crump was the president of the CPR from 1955 to 1974.)

17.   Jack Lillicio – Family Name

My Dad never knew this fact because he died when he was 62, but I learned it later in life. Our family name goes back to Venice maybe 1600. They were all tea merchants, and things went sour in the tea business so they moved to Scotland and England, and they made a fortune. Prior to the Boston Tea Party they had a feud and that section of the family sailed off for Boston and lost everything, and they moved North Carolina, and got kicked out of the US because they were Empire Loyalists, and settled in Peterborough and Toronto, and all the time my father, who was born in Scotland and came over in 1908, and his Dad was the Ridgeways Tea merchant, blended all the tea in Vancouver.

So that's a little bit about my family.

18.   Brenda Casey – Another First for Me

I went to the University of Winnipeg and ended up being the Dean of Women there, in my fourth year of university. I had been working at the university in the summers as well, and had done some teaching for seminar groups in the collegiate section that was affiliated with the university.

They decided they wanted to experiment. There was a wonderful president in place at the time, who had very innovative ways of thinking, and he felt that somebody who was closer to the age of the students that were there would have more opportunity of finding out some of the issues that students were struggling with, so that they could either seek out counselling, or seek academic assistance in an easier fashion, rather than having to demonstrate the difficulty and be caught thereafter.

So he instituted a role called Dean of Women, and had me live at the university in residence. Living in residence was fun, but it wasn't something that my parents had thought would happen. Their daughters only moved out of home when they got married.

My mother girded her loins and at least could say, "My daughter's Dean of Residence at the University of Winnipeg, and that's why she moved out." It was very hard for her.

Living in residence was part and parcel of the job, because there were a number of girls living in the residence as well who were living there because their homes were further away, or they were from out of town.

It was next to the boys' residence, and there was no Dean of Boys' Residence, so I was also there for the boys. I think in some ways I had trained to be a councellor in my youth because I listened to my mother a lot. I had home schooling that way. This was very helpful in assisting me to clarify what issues people had in private that manifested themselves in public. A lot of the young girls would confide in me and I'd direct them to appropriate resources. Some of the young boys did, too.

We were all of the same age, 18 and up, and I was only 21.

One of the kids that was most seriously affected was a boy who was self damaging. He would swallow open safety pins, and come and tell me after he had done that. So I would go with him to the hospital and they would have to be surgically removed. Again, being young, I didn't really know what to do about it. He had a psychiatrist who obviously didn't know what to do about it either.

I remember that being a major problem. There were other kids who did some self-damaging things.

The other thing about being Dean of Women was that the president of the university and a lot of the administration would come over for coffee and wine and cheese, and that was something a 21-year-old girl having these opportunities was exceptional in my circle.

I was put in positions where I had to be much more grown up than I thought I really was, so I learned how to function in circumstances that were not my norm. I think that was helpful for me in the longer term.

19. Hal Giles – Fire Tower

My daughter, Christa, in Vancouver sent out something on Facebook asking her acquaintances to tell her something they had done that they think no one else in her acquaintance would have done. My contribution is that I was part of a crew that built an 80-foot steel fire tower in Quebec in the summer of 1961. It was part of working for the Ottawa River Forest Protection Association Limited. They were an amalgamation looking after fire protection for a group of logging companies on the Quebec side of the Ottawa River.

When I arrived at this particular job the tower had been taken down from another mountain. They didn't like the location, so they had taken it down the year before. It was at the end of a lake, and we loaded all the steel into an Ottawa River boat, which was a long wooden boat with 45 degree angled sides, so the more you loaded into it the wider it got. It was very stable. An old open-flywheel motor. About four or five hours later we got up to the end of the lake. We portaged the thing maybe half a mile to another small lake and then crossed that on two canoes with poles across to make a square outrigger thing, with a small horse-and-a-half motor in one corner, but it did the job.

We got to the edge of the lake where we built a cabin for the tower operators. Then we had the process of getting the steel up the mountain. The foreman said that in enlightened days of Quebec he couldn't ask us to carry stuff on our backs, but if we wanted horses we'd have to build a road for them, so we decided to carry it.

Our shoulder pads were the old white life jackets. We cut them in half so we each had a pad to put on our shoulders and we piled the steel on that. The legs weren't too bad. They were about 6 feet long and you could carry one or two by yourself. When it got to the long diagonal brace rods, they were about 20 feet long, and they needed someone at each end with the thing bouncing up and down in the middle, so it wasn't something pleasant to carry.

I remember it was a mile and a half up the mountain to where we were putting the tower on top. The clearing had all been done the year before. We had to pack bags of powdered cement and gravel. As I remember we found water half way up where we filled fire backpacks with water to carry it up. We had to hand-mix the cement for the footings and did that first so the concrete would be set while we were packing the steel for the tower up.

The whole thing was put together with ropes and pulleys. The engineer organizing it was an interesting man to work with. He had all sorts of neat ideas how to do things. We had to dig holes down to the bedrock, which wasn't very far, maybe a foot and a half at the most to get down to solid rock. We were using sledgehammers and star drills to drill holes for anchor bolts. We worked in teams of two. One person holding the drill and the other swinging the sledgehammer. If you hit the person holding the drill you changed positions. So you had the incentive to be accurate swinging the sledgehammer.

That took several days. We'd work at that a couple of hours at a time, and then do something else.

When it came to putting the tower up, we had two legs and two cross pieces making a square, and two diagonal tie rods making an X in the middle. That was one side of the tower. We'd make one set on one side, then one set on the opposite side, then stand them up. So we had four corners and two sides built at that point, and you put the other two horizontals on and the cross pieces, and that would be the base on the footings.

Then we made a gin pole, which was just a peeled log. It was lashed at the bottom with four ropes and a block and tackle. We'd lift two of the block and tackles up on opposite corners and haul the gin pole up. Then attach the other two so the bottom was held in the middle of the tower by four block and tackles at the corners.

With ropes we could swing it to the east and the west, and pull up one section to that side, bolt it on, swing the gin pole to the other side and haul up that side. Once you had that side up, then the cross pieces went on either side.

The use of the gin pole was really an interesting thing and I'll never forget how it was done.

The rule for the people on the tower was that you checked absolutely every nut and bolt as you went up your corner. One guy missed one, and put his foot on it on the third day and it let go and he went sliding down the outside of the tower. He got to the bottom and said he wasn't going up again.

So I started on his corner at forty feet and went to the top and that was the start of my tower climbing thing.

When we got up to the top the fire towers tapered, so it was maybe 12 feet across at the bottom, and at the top it was maybe 4 feet on a side of the square. There was a square wooden thing went in the top, and I remember the foreman took up a come-along. The tower was diamond shaped because the tower had twisted. Then he took this square to get it to fit, and then he pulled up the pieces.

At that time we put a ladder up the side, so we had a ladder with hoops around it for safety up the side to a hatch in the floor of the cabin. The cabin floor got built first, and then the sides went up. There were eight sides; it was octagonal. Then pie shaped pieces went up on the roof. I remember the foreman, to get the last piece on the roof he had to be up on top of the roof and get that last piece in and come in through a hatch to get back down.

I think there were about 30 of us on the job, and it was probably three weeks before we got finished. This was in Quebec, and the foreman spoke both English and French, there was one guy younger than me who spoke only French, most people spoke both English and French, and if they spoke English it was with a French accent, so I assumed they were all French. There was a letter came in with the food supply one day, and the foreman opened it up and held it up and said, "Does anyone read French?"

I surprised everyone, because I was the only one that could read it. I realized after that most of them were rural people and probably illiterate in both languages.

20. Connor Wakelin – Camping

About two years ago I went camping with my family (minus my Mum because she couldn't get the days off work.)

When we were camping we had a trailer. It was pretty cool inside.

One time we were driving around looking around trying to go canoeing. It was pouring rain outside, but it stopped, so we went when the rain stopped. Then my Dad got an alarm on the truck saying that the tire had low air pressure. He went out there and checked, and it was fine. But it kept on saying that symbol.

So he eventually stopped at the canoeing place and it was completely pouring rain outside again; it was almost a hurricane pretty much. And it seemed that he hit a tack in the road, which popped the tire. So my Dad had to find a place to change the spare tire, which we had in the back. My Dad took a picture of that. I didn't know why.

It took about 20 minutes to drive to Kal Tire, and it took about an hour to repair, and then we got so lucky. There was a White Spot right across the street. So when we got over there my Dad got the picture and sent it to my Mum saying, "Ha, ha. Funny story."

When we finished the meal, we went over there and everything was done. Then we headed back to camp, and when we got there, there was a bunch of birds and squirrels and chipmunks everywhere around our campsite. We didn't know why, so we went over there, and we saw this peanut bag that my brother had left out. He said that he would put it inside, but he didn't.

So there was a hole in it, and all the peanuts were gone. It was a full bag when we left.

There was just a bunch of chipmunks, birds, and squirrels all around it, so it seems the birds poked a hole in it and got some peanuts out. The squirrels and chipmunks climbed up the little table and just grabbed it all.

But it was really fun when we got back.

And that's the story of my camping trip.

21. Hal Giles – Working in Quebec in the 50s

The summer of 1956 I was 14, and a friend of mine and I had been hired at a resort on White Forest lake on the Quebec side of the Ottawa River somewhere between Montreal and Ottawa, I think in the Lachine area. Couldn't find it again if I wanted to.

The idea was that one of us would work in the kitchen and the other was to work in the yard. But the way it worked out, if the resort was busy and the restaurant was full we were both in the kitchen washing dishes or whatever, and if it wasn't busy we were both out in the yard, looking after the yard. There was a boat house, recreation centre with shuffleboard and whatnot that we looked after, there was a beach. One of the things on the beach they had a black lab dog that would be wandering around in the shallows and about once a week it would catch a fish. It was quite a thing to watch.

Among other things there was a lounge in this place that was open probably every day, maybe even Sunday. We were waiting tables in this place at the age of 14. We were waiting tables when it was busy. There was a bartender in the place.

Some time during the late summer the manager and the bartender had an argument, and I'm not sure whether the bartender quit or was fired, but he was gone. The manager decided it was too late in the summer to get another one in, so he was going to tend bar himself on the Friday and Saturday nights when it was busy. He decided that we had been working in the bar, waiting tables and that, so we could look after it when it wasn't busy in the middle of the week. So between my friend and I we took turns tending bar. We had a Bartender's Bible; if someone asked for something, we had all the mixings there, and we'd make it.

Part of our jobs also during the early part of the summer was to scrub the place out on Sunday morning. After Saturday night we had to put all the chairs up and do the floors and that. We had access to things like the key to the juke box, so we could open it up and play all the tunes for free while we were working in there. Fats Domino's "Blueberry Hill" was popular that summer among other things.

We also had access to everything in the bar. Well, neither of us even drank beer at that time, but we had started off early in the summer making a version of lemonade that was an ounce of lemon juice and fruit sugar that you use for mixing drinks, then fill it up with soda water. As the summer went on we cut down on the fruit sugar and got to the point where we were drinking an ounce of lemon juice filled up with soda water.

We were so young, and we were mixing drinks behind the bar, and people were wanting to buy us a drink, and we used to mix up one of these and say, "Here, drink one of mine, and I'll drink one of yours."

Well, we were used to these things, but they couldn't stand them. So we never had to sample any of theirs.

The other thing that was there was a gas pump. And I mean a gas pump. It was one of the old ones that had a lever on the side. You physically wobbled this lever back and forth and you pumped gas from a tank, up into a glass at the top that was measured. Generally it was boat gas that we were selling. You used the nozzle to fill the can, and it measured down from the top so you knew how much you were giving them.

The one other thing, it was at a big lake, and people had boats. One day a sailboat tied up at the wharf. A five-year-old kid came up with money in his hand, "My dad wants three beers, open them please, my Dad doesn't have an opener. So we did that, and we gave the kid three beers and he walked outside, stood out in front of the picture window. He drained one, put the empty on the windowsill, and took the other two down to his Dad.

The Quebec Provincial Police dropped in every once in a while, but they were like everybody else; they wanted their beer, so that was normal, and that was just life in Quebec.

In Ontario there were beer parlours that women couldn't go into. A couple of years later, when I was in New Brunswick, you could go to the Boat Club if you had a membership, and get alcohol, and I think the Beaverbrook Hotel had a lounge. Other than that, if you were old enough you could buy your liquor at the beer store and the liquor outlet and drink it at home, but legally you couldn't serve it to a visitor. You could only drink in your own home.

Quebec had a more tolerant view.

4. The Old Days in British Columbia

1. Roz Giles– Coming to B. C.

Hal had been dating a woman in Ottawa, and I knew I wasn't the only one. But I got nominated to be one of the high school princesses so I was obliged to go to the dance. He had already invited the other one, promised her that he would be taking her to the Grade 12 dance, and there I was, left hanging. I had to ask a guy to take me to the dance. It was awful. He was a nice guy, but I was stranded.

So I gave Hal his walking ticket.

So we went through a summer, sort of, but somewhere along the line he saw the error of his ways, and ditched the one in Ottawa, but I've never forgiven him the business of that dance.

I was raised in the town of Almont Ontario, which is near Ottawa. I grew up on a farm until my last year of school, which was Grade 12, and I went to work in the Bank of Canada for about 6 ½ years while Hal went off to University at Fredericton, New Brunswick.

We had come to the end of his years in University, he'd given me an engagement ring for Christmas that year, so that was kind of in the plans. The only problem was that he had missed a couple of papers in his last year of university. I think it was too much Drama Club and Radio Club and just enjoying life instead of concentrating on his studies, but the decision was still made. I had three or four thousand dollars saved. We would get married, but where would he go to look for work? I wasn't thinking of working. I was getting married for heaven's sakes!

It happened that a chap was home from Prince George. We had been debating, out West or up North, maybe, in the camps. Hal's Dad said, "Why don't you go talk to him, and see what he says about Prince George?"

So this guy kindly gave us his time. He said, "If you can't find work in Prince George, you might as well go shoot yourself." This was 1965, and they were building three pulp mills in Prince George, so it was a boom town, and that certainly sounded more attractive than a small bush camp in Northern Ontario.

So we made our plans, got married on June 12 and very shortly thereafter we loaded all our belongings in our half-ton truck and headed west. Hal's parents had given us a 9 X 9 canvas tent, not the lightest thing in the world compared to today's equipment, but that was in the back of our pickup, and we camped our way across Canada. I vividly remember one night on the shores of Lake Superior in a provincial park. It was pouring rain, a thunderstorm, I think, and we had to try and haul this canvas tent out of the back of the truck, not touching it too much, or it would leak, and set up our camp. Bear in mind I had never been a camper. Hal's family was, but our farm had Holstein cows that liked to be milked twice a day, so we had not been a family that took many holidays.

So the camping was pretty new to me.

We got to Prince George safe and sound, though we claimed we'd never seen any mountains. We came in through the Pine Pass from Edmonton, and down the highway from there, and it had been foggy all the way down, and we didn't see the tops of the mountains at all. It was a little bit hairy.

But we got to Prince George, and we were looking for a place to live, but it was a boom town, remember? All the hotels and motels and everything available were pretty well taken, except for one little room in a seedy motel at the bottom of the Hart Highway where when you opened the door you could smell the stink of the water pipes. It was not pleasant, but it was a dry bed and it wasn't a tent, so we happily took up residence there.

Hal very quickly the next day was down to se the EI people or whatever they call that place these days, and very quickly got a job, not in one of the mills, but surveying the Hydro line between Prince George and Endako. So I was in the motel and getting to know somebody down the road, I recall, and he went out to the bush the next day, and he didn't come home, and he didn't come home, and he still didn't come home long past the time when I really was expecting him to be home.

A kind soul – I think she was from Niagara Falls – down the way in the motel, we must have chatted about what was going on to some extent, and somewhere along seven or eight o'clock she came around with a rum and coke for me, and said, "I think maybe you need this."

Talk about making friends quickly. It was wonderful.

Anyway, Hal eventually arrived with a long story about kinda missing where he was supposed to meet the rest of the group, and we went on from there. We very quickly got into an apartment, because somebody got evicted that night and we just happened to show up at the door, and since then life's been pretty good to us.

56

2. Roz Giles – Camp in the Sukunka

The year was 1972 and I had been hired as the camp cook for my husband's small crew of six men doing volume and decay surveys for the Forest Service. It was kinda like feeding the family almost. We had daughter Heather at that stage, and she would have been two years old.

The crew, being the nice sorts that they were, led by Gordon Long, had built a little sand box for Heather out in the yard.

The crew's living quarters and dining room, and the cook trailer formed a T-shape, and the sand box was just at the end of the T, just a little piece out, but still where I could keep an eye on her.

One day, the crew had come in, and Tom came to me, saying, "Roz, have you seen my glasses around. I can't find my glasses. I wondered whether Heather has taken them."

I said, "I don't know, but I'll ask her." So I had Heather, I was down on my knees face to face with her, saying, "Heather, where have you put Tom's glasses?"

She wasn't giving me the right answer. She was facing me, and I had my back to the sandbox. She kept saying, it sounded like, "Bear, bear."

I said, "No, glasses."

And then Gordon came along and tapped me on the shoulder and said, "Roz, you might want to take Heather inside."

I said, "Why?"

He said, "Well, there's a bear out in the sand box."

Well, I did take Heather inside, and thanks to Gord's wise council, we were all safe, and Gord dispatched the bear to a nicer place.

3. Roz Giles – The Flying Sailboat.

1971 and we were still in the camp at Chetwynd where I was the camp cook and Hal was the boss of the small crew. We had a Volkswagen Beetle at that stage that was our family car. For some reason or other it had the boat on top of it. Hal had probably had it out doing some fishing. He had untied it with the intention of taking it off and storing it so I could go to town. Then he got called off to something more urgent than taking the boat off the car, and I just needed to get to town, and away I went, boat on top.

It was making a little bit of racket I guess as I drove around, because it was a gravel road. And then I realized that there wasn't any racket happening. I stopped and looked up. No boat. So I headed back to camp to give Hal the bad news. His immediate reaction was that it would probably be smashed to smithereens if it had come off. We went back to have a look, hopefully to find it, but I had come back and had not seen it.

However, it was in the ditch. It had survived with maybe just a wee chunk of paint off. It had gracefully floated off the top of the car and floated into the ditch. It was bottom up in perfect shape otherwise.

4.   Tom Brown – Trip to Quesnel

The two of us we loaded up in this car and took off. We got as far as Hope. At that time there was a toll on the highway there, and we just got past it a little ways, and it had been pouring rain and we hit a huge puddle of water. It stalled the car, and we couldn't get it going, so we had to stay for the night. We looked around and there was an Indian shack there, I guess cause they had fishing stations around there. So we went over and climbed into that.

Boy, we weren't there long and we were itching, itching. And I think we had a flashlight or maybe a match, and we looked and we were just black with mosquitoes. So we had to come back to the car.

We had to wait until morning. Finally a truck or somebody came along and gave us a tow and got us going. So we drove then up to just past Spence's Bridge, going up by Ashcroft, and up the hill there, just valleys of tomatoes, as far as you could see.

By then the sun was out, and we went and picked a few each. We had to walk down, we came back and we were standing behind the car eating them, when a police car pulled up behind us. "What are you doing? Where did you get the tomatoes?"

We said, "We just picked them."

"Well, that's stealing."

Anyways, to make a long story short, he said, "Follow me into town."

So we followed him down into Ashcroft. He said, "You go in there and stay. The judge will be out in a minute."

We went in there, scared to death, and pretty soon this guy said, "Okay, come on."

So we went out and the judge was there, and he said, "That's a pretty serious thing you boys, stealing and that."

Anyways, he fined us. I think because we were panicky when they stopped us and talked to us, and I think he must have looked in our wallets, because he fined us all the money we had, and left us with nothing.

I was complaining about this. He said, "Well, if you don't want to pay the fine, you can go to jail." He said, "Maybe you should go and look at the jail."

So we did. Boy, that was just solid cement there. So we decided, what the heck, we'd pay the fine.

Of course then we didn't have any money, so we were bumming around there, didn't know what to do. So we were stealing tomatoes and stuff and living. Finally we went up to Ashcroft Manor and knocked on the door and asked the lady there if she needed any help, and she said, "No."

"Well, can we work for food?"

She said, "Yeah, yeah, there's a pile of wood."

After that we split the wood and really worked hard, and pretty soon she hollered us in, and when we went in she asked us "what are you kids doin' up here anyways?"

So we told her our story.

She laughed. "That was a policeman. There's no judge here. They just did that for a party. They're out partyin' with that money."

Anyways, then it worked out not too bad, I guess, because she knew the owner of the TU Auto Court, there, and she said, "I'll phone him and see, he can probably use somebody."

I told her that I did mechanic work, and I got a job there, and Ab, she gave him a job at her place, so we both worked there and after I don't know how long we got some money and we come back down again.

But when we come down June (my fiancée) went back up there. Her brother Ab, he went back to work there, and June, she went with him and waited tables for a while, and then she cooked there at Ashcroft Manor after that. We never did get to Quesnel.

5. Tom Brown – Married Life

My wife's folks moved out to the top of the hill out 72nd above us. There were 4 girls in their family and one boy. As soon as they moved out they started going to the Langley School. To do that they walked down the hill right past our road.

The first time I met them I didn't know who they were. They went down and they registered, and they took the kids. At that time they had a team of horses and a covered wagon that they'd used back in the Prairies that they'd used to go to school. We were quite surprised at this wagon comin' up the road there, and we were in the ditch playin' – that's what she told me later – we were playing back and forth and such, and we were all red haired in our family, and those folks were sayin' "I wonder who those red-haired kids belong to."

Anyways it was no time until we got to know them, because we'd walk down the hill in a crowd. From her place, they were the farthest away from the school. By the time they got down to our road there were probably 10 or 20 kids. Then we'd all walk all the way down to Langley. Up 72nd we were about two miles and she was another half a mile. The school was at 200th and Fraser Highway.

But with kids, because there was a gang, we were playing and the distance didn't matter.

Right away we got to know one another, so goin' home at night they'd always at least two in the Skelton family would come to our place and two of our kids would go up to her place. It was the girls. They always seemed to be at our place.

About that time she had an older sister and another friend of mine, he was dating her, and he had a car – he was older than I was and he had a car – so we started then and we'd go to shows and dances and stuff, and he dated Ona, my wife's older sister and I took June, and we'd go together. It was a Model A Ford with a rumble seat, so in the good weather her and I could sit in the back, and the bad weather we'd sit in the front and she sat on my knee.

So we went to shows and stuff. I wasn't thinking at all about getting' married when I went overseas but you know being that she was always at our place, and we always went together and everything, and when I went overseas she always wrote me when I was there, and when we came back it seemed to be the thing to do. Just get married and settle down.

So that's how I met her. She was 7 and I was 9 when they moved out here.

For the honeymoon we went over to Victoria, and then you had to get on the boat at 9 o'clock and it took all night, at least I think they tied up, you were on all night, and you got off at Victoria at 7 in the morning. So we drove up island, and we ended up having quite a quiet time. There was no excitement on our honeymoon. It was pretty routine.

6.   Alan Brown– Early Days in B. C.

I was born here, out of Langley Parish, I guess, in 1932. At that time I guess there was lots of snow around, two or three feet of snow. They didn't have no way of getting a doctor or anything, so there was a midwife coming when I was born. I guess they had quite a time, because I came through all right.

I went to school here in Langley for I forget how many years.

Then we moved away from there over Willoughby, and we went to school there when I was growing up. Then we left there and went to Saturna Island. We lived on Saturna Island and went to school up there. I only got to Grade 6. I didn't get very far in school.

Then when I finished school we came down, I went to work in the sawmill for a while, and then Tom he started logging, and I went up logging with Tom, and stayed with Tom for quite a few years. It was more building logging roads.

I was in logging pretty well all my life.

7.   Marg Kennet – Growing Up in B. C.

My maiden name was Peachey, and I wasn't too happy having that as a maiden name. For 24 years of my maiden life it was just a pain. "Peachy keen," etcetera, etcetera. Nobody could spell it. It was Peachey, but they would leave the "y" off. And anyway it was an interesting name.

I was born in Victoria, and my parents shortly before then got married in 1943 in Blind Bay.

My parents were both raised in the North Okanagan, my dad in Canoe and my Mom in Blind Bay. I was born in Victoria and my Dad worked in the shipyard as a pipefitter and my Mom stayed home. I lived in Victoria for the first five years of my life and I was an only child. So it was kinda lonely, because there was only one other girl on the street in those five years. Her name was Nancy, and I can't really think of any connection that we had.

So I didn't have a lot of playmates.

But anyhow, when I was about 5 my Dad decided that he wanted to go back to the Okanagan. He missed the orchard and the farm-type life. They just had a mixed farm, his folks, but he missed that type of lifestyle, so up we went. And we actually lived in a very beautiful place. We leased an orchard between Blind Bay and Sorento on Shuswap lake. It was a 10-acre apple orchard and the house was a beautiful Tudor-style English home. The people had died and someone was needed to care for this property, so the timing was perfect, and that's where we landed. I was 5.

The winters were pretty awful up there, and not like it is up there now. It would get to be 40 degrees below and we would have up to 110 inches of snow per year. And the mail would come over

Shuswap Lake on the ice, and the ice was very interesting. We lived near the lake, and at night I could hear the ice cracking and it just does that. It's an eerie sound, and then I could hear the coyotes chasing the deer. And that made me sad because I knew that the deer was going to be the loser.

The ice didn't go out on the lake until the end of April, so that's a long, hard winter, and we did not have a car.

So then spring came and that meant that Mum and Dad were very busy in the orchard because they tried not to hire folk, because that was expensive.

I've got to say one more thing about the winter. The winter was interesting because in the garage of this really interesting property, I found a pair of adult skis that were probably about six feet high. I was determined that I was going to ski down this hayfield that we had. I didn't have much else to do. There were no ski boots, so I strapped these to my boots and I fell so many times, and of course the snow would develop a crust and be really, really hard, and when you fell on crust you got a lot of road rash. Your face and anything else that was exposed.

I finally perfected the art of skiing with these crazy skis, so wintertime was kind of fun, but then springtime with the orchard all in bloom was pretty wonderful and under the trees grew asparagus and that was just something that we all looked forward to. It was just growing wild and it was beautiful and it was wonderful and tasty.

Then I would go out with Mum with a Rogers Syrup can and I would go up into the field and I would look for wild strawberries, because they taste so good. There's nothing like a wild strawberry. They're teenie weenie but they're so tasty. I would try and get as many of those as I could.

We had chickens. We would get the chickens, probably in late winter. It was a big farm kitchen, and we'd have these little chicks corralled off in the kitchen until they were old enough to go into the barn and the henhouse. And I would collect the eggs. I liked doing that. And we had a couple of cows and we had geese. One gander, I was just petrified of. He'd bite me. You know the wingspan of those things is huge. He didn't like me one bit, so he used to take after me, but one Christmas he was Christmas dinner, so that was that.

Then when I was about twelve, I guess, Dad gets the idea that we're going to go back to Victoria. About 1953, so we'd been up there about four years, Dad bought this car. A Morris Minor. What would possess anybody to buy a Morris Minor when they have a farm? He needed to buy a truck. Anyway he didn't. So we had this Morris Minor, and then when we were coming to Victoria he bought an International truck, built a canopy on it, and because everything was furnished where we lived, he just put the necessities in there, and so off we came. We were headed for Victoria.

Mom was very fond of this canary. We were all sitting in the front, and Mum had this canary on her lap, and the canary was about to have a heart attack any minute I was sure. We had friends in the Fraser Valley, so we stopped there the night, and that's when I first saw TV, and I remember "Oklahoma!" Was on.

Well, I couldn't believe it. We left the canary there. Mum's heart was broken, but it was pretty obvious that the canary was not going to survive the rest of the trip, so we left the canary.

Then in Victoria we settled in Brentwood Bay, and that's where I stayed for the rest of my growing years until I was 20 and had two years at UVic, and then came over to UBC. But that's another story I guess.

5. Family Lore

What is it like to sit down of and evening and listen when these families get going?

Badayev Family

Alex Badayev, Olena Chemeris, and their daughter Yuliya Badeyeva emigrated to Tsawwasen from Ukraine in 2003.

1.   Alex Badayev - My Younger Years

We lived in the centre of Kiev. I was born in 1954, and I remember when I was really young we lived in a communal apartment for almost 6 years. I don't remember much. It was a big, old house built before the Revolution in 1916. It was a big apartment, probably 3000 square feet, and after the Revolution it was divided into small rooms. They would keep the kitchen, and they would divide all the other space into rooms. So people lived in these rooms, and everybody would use one kitchen and shower and washroom. Six or seven families.

Then we moved to a separate apartment in the centre of Kiev. But those years we were in such a community in the 1960s where there were a lot of gangs. Small gangs. It was like in New York, with the kid's gangs. But small gangs. Not the kind of gangs with guns. There were no guns at that time. But they can punch you and take money from you.

I experienced that sometimes. I remember when I was eight years old, one of the gang members – I remember this very clearly – he said something bad to me. A bad word. He was ten and I was eight. I was standing at one side of the courtyard, and he was up on the balcony on the other side. I picked up a stone and threw it. It hit him directly on the temple.

He fell down immediately, with a lot of blood. Everybody came.

After this accident, I was a very respected guy. Everybody respected me.

My father was born in Sochi in the Caucasus in Russia. He was a southern guy, not Chechyen, but close. My family name is like a Chechyen family name, but it is Russian. He has a very hot temper. And I also, and Yuliya, too. So we are very impulsive.

When somebody provokes me, I will reply immediately, so they discovered that, and so I got respect. It was the same in school, because I went to school where students were from very respected families of Kiev. From government guys. So for example, one of our teachers was the wife of the Secretary of the Communist Party of the Ukraine. So in our school there was a lot of sons and daughters of very high people.

I was there because my Mum wanted me to start English at an early age, and she had contacts because she was a well-known doctor. She knew people.

Olena: I'm from a middle-class family. My father was an engineer. I grew up in a middle-class neighbourhood. My childhood was average. Alex doesn't accept it, but he was privileged. He was one or two levels up. His Dad was the director of a big gas institute, taking care of all the gasoline and pipelines.

Alex: My mother was a very respected doctor.

Olena: So they had access to everything.

Alex: But when I went to this school, I was below the other students. They were the top, but I felt that I was below the others. They were the elite of the Ukraine. But then I got friends. But I did not spend a lot of time with them. I started sports. Professional sports.

In Grade 8 I became a professional at pentathlon. I did that for two years. I practiced every day for 5 hours, because I had five different sports. Fencing and swimming and running one day. The next day horse riding and shooting.

It was very hard for me. It was a great deal of exercise. Then I left and went to professional fencing, and I got very good results, and I have a Masters of Sport in fencing.

And that was all after school. I was in Grade 10 when I left Pentathlon and took up fencing. I studied the Sciences. I was completely busy all day long. Until three o'clock I was in school, then two hours for my home exercises, then I went to practice until 10 o'clock. Then 10 hours I slept, then back to school, every day.

I was so busy that I did not have a social life, but I enjoyed this, so I did not spend a lot of time with these high-class guys, drinking and smoking and everything. But I was a strong guy and I remember, if you take into account all my classmates, the top ones, I don't know where they are. They are just gone. Maybe three or five of them have even died. Because they had everything. They just spent time drinking and smoking, and that's all.

65

We had 20 – 25 pupils in each class. We had very good Math and very good Physics teaching. We were very strong, and most of all very strong in languages. I was very strong compared to students in other schools, because I was very good in grammar.

When we came here, I was the only one speaking English. Only me. But right now, I am on the same level as the rest of the family.

2. *Alex Badayev – Vacation in Gurzuf*

In Crimea, for example, Gurzuf, it was the young people's resort. They all came to Gurzuf, and in summer we would spend three months there, holidaying, drinking, meeting girls. That was when I was in high school and university, and when I was twenty years old, until I was thirty-three years old. Every summer we went there. When I was working it was just a month or a month and a half.

3. *Alex Badayev – Breakup of the Soviet Union.*

When it happened, I was thinking, "Was it good, or was it bad?"

Ukraine became independent. I was thinking it was better to separate from the Soviet Union, because Russia is so big. Maybe Moscow, St. Petersburg, yes, I would be closer to them. But I would like to be separated from the other parts of Russia, from the middle parts of Russia, from such countries as Chechnya and Turkistan, which are different countries.

I was thinking the economical potential of the Ukraine was great at the time, because it had everything: metallurgical, agricultural. Agriculture is absolutely beautiful in Ukraine. No comparison with any other country because we have such beautiful soil. We have the best sugar in the world. Ten Ukrainian sugar production plants have recently been bought by German companies.

Ukraine had a very good starting opportunity. It had much greater opportunity than Poland, for example. Poland was a very poor country. I was thinking, "It will be okay. I will start my own business, and I will be successful."

But then twenty-five years of doing nothing. In the same position it was 25 years ago. For us it was not so much the collapse of the Soviet Union. I predicted this because for two years before the Soviet Union collapsed it was already different in the republics.

I remember I was really encouraged. I was really inspired at what was going on in Moscow and St. Petersburg.

There was a new stock market in Moscow, but I was back and forth to Moscow, and I was making a lot of money, because I was buying a lot of goods in Moscow, and selling them in Ukraine. Moscow had a lot of money, and there was great opportunity there.

4.   Olena Chemeris – Coming to Canada

I was working after my maternity leave. I came back to work and by that time Yuliya went to school, and it was a beautiful school. A special school in Kiev. Beautiful kids, beautiful teacher, beautiful parents. We all lived close by. We raised the children so we knew each other since they were born. We were walking with the strollers, and then we went to kindergarten, and then we went to school, so it was like one big family. Not as close as family, but it was one big group of kids and parents. So it was really great.

Then my job. I worked at the bank. It was a similar situation. When I was in university it was the Soviet Union. At that time the Soviet Union collapsed, and it opened doors to business, to all sorts of commerce, like business opportunities never known before. We used to have only Government banks, like national banks, and here go commercial banks, and they would pay a good salary, and it was a great opportunity.

It's the same story. I would study at university with a group of friends and then we would go after graduation we would go to the same bank. It was a young bank, a young crowd, all friends. It was just great.

After maternity leave I went back to work and I got promotions one after the other. It was just opportunities were open in front of me. I had a great family. I had friends, I had my Mum. She would come after school and she would pick Yuliya up and take her to swimming or take her to art classes, or take her somewhere else. I would come home, and we lived with Alex's Mum. I would work from nine to six, I would come home at six thirty, and dinner was ready, Alex was fed, because Alex's Mum was there.

So it was all settled. A good life. And when our friends started moving to Canada, I remember, even Alex was saying, "No I'm not going to go." But at one point I understand that business got to the point where he changed his mind, and he decided to leave. I didn't want to leave. I had a perfect life. Our apartment was very close to downtown. Close to everything. I had everything. Maybe I wanted a little bit more, but I hoped it would come. But in general, I was raised this way. We never talked about leaving the country. So I never ever pictured myself living somewhere else and leaving my parents and leaving my friends. It was a huge stress. It was bad, and

I had an ulcer, and I think that stress contributed to my ulcer, because it was very stressful.

I know that Alex is a very persistent person, and I didn't have any chance. You know if you heard, I called myself a "Decembrist wife." It was back in Tsar's times, back in Russia a couple of centuries ago, there were rebels, and the Tsar sent them to Siberia, and their wives followed them, and they lived with them and shared that struggle and hardship. It happened in December, so they were called Decembrists. It was total dedication. The wives changed their luxury life in St. Petersburg for a modest life in Siberia.

But I called myself a Decembrist wife because I followed my husband into exile in Tsawwassen.

But Alex has a very strong personality, and I know he told me, "We will just go. We will see how it goes. We always have the chance to come back." But in the back of my mind that slight chance of coming back was very slim. But still I was hoping that we still could get an opportunity to come back.

So that's what happened.

Then we got here, and honestly, I thought, "Okay, Alex. You brought me here. I'm not going to do anything. You brought me here. You pay for my life. You have to support me." I went to school to study English at VCC. I'm grateful that our friends suggested that this was a great place, and I think it's the best place to learn English.

And then we met one couple who are Americans who live in Point Roberts. She's Russian and he's American. Alex met the husband at Winskill in the swimming pool. So we became friends, and on day, she was saying, "My husband's sister was asking if I have someone who is looking for a part-time job at some dairy close by."

I'm like, "I don't know. Alex, what should I do?"

So I went, "Okay part time job, pocket money." I don't want to have to tell Alex what I have to buy. I wanted independence. I was always independent, and that was important to me.

I went for an interview. They were probably so desperate. They needed people. So it was a five-minute interview at the front door, and it was around 10 am, and they asked, "Can your start at 2?"

So I started at 2. My English was like Julia's, like "Mother, Father, sister, brother, I was born in Kiev, I graduated from..." and that's it. And I remember it was a simple job in the dairy plant. I had to put bottles on the conveyor, working on the factory floor. When they couldn't explain to me what to do, they would just show me. They would hold my hand and show me what to do.

But actually Olympic is where I picked up my English. Because whatever school you go to and however long you study, it's only being in the environment that will help you to learn English. So the first three years were tough, very tough. I still don't like to recall these times. Even though I was younger, It was still not good, it's tough times for me.

We even had friends who would speak English, but sometimes people who speak your language, it's not quite the same. So it's very important to have people who have the same view and you enjoy being with.

I would say that three years was the first break point for me. After three years I started feeling confident. That was after three years. I felt confident being an immigrant here. Before that I would be horrified in stores, at the till, because the cashiers always want to talk to you, and I was horrified sometimes. I would just put on a stupid smile, and "Ha, ha" and "I don't know what she was asking me." Or later on I would think, "Oh, that's what she was asking me."

We used to go to Commercial Drive on weekends. They have those European stores, and the Italian market would have a variety of cheeses and salami. And at that place, you had to tell exactly what you want. "I want six varieties of different...something." For me it was a challenge, a real challenge. I was almost shaking when I was waiting in line, to say, "Can I get 100 grams of cheese." It was horrifying. But I passed that. I survived.

I would say that three years was the big break. Then it's been progressively better. I moved to the office. There was an opening position, and my supervisor told me, "You can apply for that position." I always told them that I wanted to work in the office, and if they had a position I would take it.

That was also challenging. It's different English. It's not only speaking, it's writing, it's emails. Now it's emails, and it's not just, "Yes," or "No." You have to explain. I always admired people who would speak nicely with beautiful English, or write beautiful emails. I just enjoy reading them. I always wanted to write emails like them. I couldn't, and probably I still can't. I notice, but I always try to kind of take something from someone else's email.

What I notice, I told Julia, is that I always try hard, and other immigrants try hard to put very smart words into emails. But

Canadians use simple words. They use simple words, but they know how to put them together, and it makes beautiful English.

Alex: Right now I have a lot of businesses with people from US, from Canada, from China. A lot of emails, and every day I am seeing different words I don't understand. Today I got an email from the US. This is a broker. He wrote me a message. "Please overnight me the bill of lading." What does it mean? Just to send in an overnight delivery. I realized this, but I would never, ever use this word."

Olena: I also find this is a beauty of English. One word, you can use as a noun, adjective, verb. Modern English is very flexible. They use "overnight" and you understand it.

Alex: In Russian, you have to write a lot of words for only one word in English.

The first breaking point was after three years, and the second major breaking point was after we bought this house after five years. Because living in an apartment, I didn't want to stay there. I wanted to be away somewhere. With friends, on the beach, just somewhere, I don't know, in the mountains. After we bought this house, I got this feeling that we had planted our roots. Now we are here for a long time. It turned everything around. You have your roots here. You have your roots and it's a big difference.

Alex: I know the third point. When I bought you a Mercedes.

Olena: It feels good, driving a Mercedes.

Julia: My bum feels warm in the morning when I get dropped off in Ladner to go to school.

Olena: Everybody loves it.

5.   Alex Badayev – Coming to Canada.

My history is that I really hated the Soviet system from the very beginning of my life. They pushed me to become a Pioneer in Grade 3, and I had to go marching with everybody. The Soviet Union would like to put everybody in the same line. Everybody should be equal. For me it was impossible. I need independence for my whole life. So I hated the Soviet system from the very beginning.

But I was a very good student in school. In University I was an excellent student. I realized I needed to be a professional. But then after graduation from University, I became a scientist in a research lab. From the very beginning I started working in a research lab. It was very interesting for me, but there was no opportunity for higher goals. You can go higher, but no opportunity unless you were a member of the Communist Party. For me it was absolutely impossible to become a member of the Party.

Actually I had a very good life in the Soviet Union, because I became a Doctor of Science, a PhD, but all my whole life I was independent. I had independent research work. I did what I wanted to. But there were no opportunities.

And then I saw my friends who were just doing some small business that was illegal in the Soviet Union. Selling something commercial, but it was illegal. But I was a respectable scientist, and I got ten times less money than my friends, who were just selling stuff.

Julie: It's the same still. Scientists with PhDs...

Alex: So they had cars, and I didn't have anything. Then I applied to the US Embassy to go to the US. In 1987 I had an interview at the US Embassy, and I got a status of Certificate of Support. It means that you need to get a sponsorship from a US citizen, and then you could immigrate. But then after Gorbachev came to power, businesses began to develop, and I realized that something changed, and I just started my business. I left the old Science, and I started business, with computers and so on. Technological business, selling computers and software. I was writing software and selling it. I saw the opportunities. I saw what was going on in Moscow. People became millionaires in one, two, three months. It was encouraging.

Just remember that those guys who were millionaires in Russia are now in jail, or killed.

So I started a business, and I was a successful businessman. I had my own driver. I had a really big business in the Ukraine. Olena got a salary from the bank, but I didn't know how much. For me it did not matter, because it was her pocket money. Three or four hundred dollars. I was buying everything. We would travel in Europe and everywhere. Yuliya was little, so Olena's parents would watch her, and we would take off to Italy, to Paris.

We travelled a lot. We had a lot of money. It was from 1993 to 2000. I had a very good business. But then after that I reached a certain level, and a lot of guys from the government came to me and said, "Hey, you are a rich guy. Share the money with us." So I paid one, and I realized how much I had to earn to support all these government guys. This was corruption.

They were threatening me. I got called from the authorities, from the prosecutor's office. They could come to my plant – I had small plants producing casings – and they could come to my plant and say, "This is bad, this is bad. You can go to jail or pay money."

Then I realized that it was impossible. The only opportunity for me was to get elected into the government, in the legislature. Why do people in the Ukraine go to the legislature? Just to save their business. The only reason you go to parliament is to secure your business, if you have a big business. All the people I knew who had influence, I knew five or six elected friends. They told me, "Yes, we are also thinking about it. But right now, we got elected, so we're safe. We can save our business."

And then I decided. No, I did not need to do that. I decided to leave. To become a software programmer and to build a new life here.

I predicted that there would be something bad in the Ukraine, and you see.

Olena: I remember Alex always said that the eastern part of the Ukraine would want to separate.

Alex: After that, this guy from Donetsk came to power, but we were already here.

So, yeah. That was my reason for coming. Because I hated the Soviet Union, and nothing has changed since. The system is still there. In Russia it's getting worse and worse. They are going back to the Soviet Union.

6. Yuliya Badayeva – Coming to Canada

I don't remember a lot but from the details that I do remember was first coming to Canada, I think it was summer after Grade 3, so I must have been turning 8. 2002.

We had come because my godfather was living here. He helped us to tour around. He took us around some places. I have such a bad memory now.

We were there for a month, and to go around the area, we rented a car. At one point we were staying in the motel on 12th Avenue down by the beach in Tsawwassen.

Olena: We came for a month to stay in Tsawwassen. We rented an apartment at Century Village Apartments, but we had to stay one or two nights until it was vacant.

Yuliya: So then we moved into the apartment and we were staying there, and I don't remember a lot, but I remember being in Canada and thinking, "Oh, this is a nice country, not so different from the Ukraine," and just kind of being clueless.

I honestly don't remember being told we were going to stay in Canada.

The following September (2003) we came here and we were staying at the Century Village Apartments again, the same place we stayed the first time. I guess we liked it there.

School was really different. I remember vividly on my first day of classes being very confused. I remember being so sad after my Mum dropped me off, and then she left, and I was like, "Noooo."

My English was not good at all. I had taken English classes in Grade One, Two and Three. I did pretty well, I think, but the extent of what they teach you in those three grades is pretty small.

I feel privileged to have gone to a pretty decent school in Kiev, capital of the country, pretty decent school, and we had a great English teacher. My cousin still takes classes from her. She had taught us as much as she could. But there's a limit to how much a kid could learn English in Grades One to Three. I think the extent was, the alphabet, I remember knowing words like Mom, Dad, grandmother, cat, dog, things like that. But not sentences.

I specifically remember that everyone was open and friendly, but I think it was pretty unusual for someone from Ukraine to come to Tsawwassen. I was the only person. I think in my whole elementary school there were two or three exchange students, and it was very rare for something of this sort to happen, and looking back on this, now, in the past year I discussed this with my close friends – I'm still really close with my friends from Elementary School – and they were like, "Yeah, we were all kind of like, 'what is this girl doing here? What's going on?'" I think everyone was just intrigued, like "what is this thing here?"

So I remember vividly on my first day of Grade 4 when I got there everyone was open and friendly, and people were asking me stuff, like, "What's your name?" trying to figure out who I am. Because the teacher probably introduced me as, like, "She's here." I don't really remember.

I had no idea what they were saying. My English wasn't good enough. I think everyone had good intentions, but that made me even more anxious and scared, because when everything is so unknown and foreign, you have to find your place, you know, in Grade 4. Everything is different. The language barrier is a big deal. I think that going through Grade 4 is tough in itself. Kids go through a lot of stuff. Do you like the school? Do you like your teachers? How are you doing in your classes? And on top of that, having a language barrier, and also not knowing customs.

I think for kids, it is important to fit in. If you don't fit in it makes school a lot harder if you don't have friends. When you don't even know how to fit in, it's just like...

So the first, I think it was two to three months of school, I was still learning English. I think it happened pretty quickly, because in Grade Five I was already in.

The reason we picked Cliff Drive was because there was ESL there. Beach Grove was closest to the apartments, but they told us Cliff Drive was where the ESL was.

I made two friends in those first five or six months. Actually I just remember having anxieties over really silly things at school, too. I remember everyone had their duo-tangs labelled, and my Mum had bought me duo-tangs, and I didn't label them, and other kids took my duo-tangs, and I just remember bawling my eyes out because "My Mum spent her money!" I knew we weren't that well off financially when we moved here, and I knew that, so I was like, "My Mum spent money and she picked nice ones, and now kids have take them."

I think the whole situation at school, I think normally I wouldn't have done that, and everyone was probably just like, "What...?"

Inevitably I was able to learn the language. I was taking ESL classes extra to my regular classes. There were a couple of other kids that were English Second Language, and we had this teacher, Miss Garden, and we did stuff. We had a salmon tank and we let them grow, and eventually we let them out somewhere into a river. That was really cool. We did a whole bunch of crossword puzzles and word searches. But I think what helped me most developing my English was that I had to know it in order to make friends, to have a normal life. That was my motivation.

Alex: At this time it was a very big risk for us to live in Tsawwassen, because there were not many immigrants and no services. But I just realized that it is the place that we must live. For the future. We needed to overcome all the difficulties, but we must live here. Whatever happened, we must. Now you see that it is okay.

7.   Olena Chemeris – One Last Good Thing About Canada

I feel protected. I feel protected here, by the government. I believe that the police will help me if I need their help. I don't know. It's so different. I feel very safe, secure and protected here. What I want to say good about the government. Because we all have times when we have to deal with the government. Like passport or driver's license or something else. If they have policy or rules, if they tell you they will send your driver's license in ten days, they will send it in ten days. And it's totally different from what we had in Ukraine. There, if you want to speed up the process, you have to have a close relationship or you have to know some guy you have to take different ways, go around, or you have to pay money.

Here, if you talk about government, you don't put equal signs between government and corruption. I feel very safe.

Alex: A good government is when you only recall the existence of government when you have to pay taxes once a year. In Ukraine you are thinking about government every day. A lot of problems come from the government.

The Long-Dev Family

Eric Long and Nini Dev married in 1996, creating a multi-ethnic extended family with a great tradition of storytelling. The following stories are approximately in chronological order.

8. *Gordon Long – Bun Smith and the 44-40*

The 44-40 was a Winchester carbine that fired .45 Colt pistol ammunition. It was handy for the cowboys and homesteaders in the old days, because they could use the same ammunition for their pistols and their rifles. It was one of the guns that won the West, and all that.

When Dad was about 12 years old, a guy called Bun Smith gave him this rifle for getting good marks in school. It was already old at that time. So this 44-40 rifle has been in the family since Dad was in school in the late 1920s.

One of my favourite stories about the 44/40 was when Dad took it back to Bun Smith to have it sighted in. Mr. Smith was an American guy who came up to homestead in the Palling area, and he was a renowned rifleman. Dad took this rifle to Bun and said, "Will you sight it in for me?"

And Bun said, "Yeah, I'll do that."

So they went out into the field. The target was already set up, and Dad said he was absolutely astounded, because Bun Smith was standing there, and Dad was just looking at him, and he suddenly dropped to the ground, flat prone, and fired three shots. "Bang, bang, bang."

Then he walked up to the target and he said, "Yeah, it's sighted a little to the left."

He tapped the sight a bit, then down on his stomach, "Bang, bang, bang."

"Right. There you are. She'll shoot straight, now."

He was just an amazing shot.

The second story that Dad told about Bun Smith was that Bun's homestead was at the end of Decker Lake. They were down at Bun's place one the winter, cutting ice from the lake, because in those days they didn't have refrigeration and everybody had an icehouse. The lake used to get about three feet thick with ice, and they would take these big crosscut saws that they generally used for cutting timber, and they would cut the blocks out. Then they would take them back to the icehouse and cover them in sawdust, and they would last pretty much all summer.

So the Long family was down cutting ice, and Bun came over and said, "There's a coyote out on the lake." Coyotes had a bounty on them in those days. This was the Depression, and nobody had much money, so if you could shoot a coyote it was pretty much worth it.

Grandpa Long said, "Yeah, okay."

And Bun said, "If you can lend me your sleigh, and young Art can drive for me, I'll go out and shoot that coyote."

So Dad takes off driving on the ice with the team of horses. And the coyote was still there. And Bun Smith is standing up with the rifle on the bed of the sleigh. He's standing up. He says, "Just keep between the coyote and the shore. Whatever you do, don't let the coyote get to the shore."

So Dad starts driving around the coyote, to herd it out onto the lake.

Bun stands up on the bed of the sleigh and starts shooting at the coyote.

Well at the first shot the horses went bonkers, and Dad doesn't say it was a runaway, but he was just able to keep the team in hand, and he kept them galloping between the coyote and the shore. And Bun hit the coyote five out of six shots. Obviously they weren't great hits, because the coyote didn't go down until the sixth one, but standing up in the bed of the sleigh with the team running wild, he hit the coyote five out of six shots.

Another story about Bun Smith I know happened for sure, because I have corroboration from more modern historical sources. There was a bank robbery in Hazleton, B. C. in April, 1914. I don't

76

know all the details about this, but the bank robbers got into the bank and then the people of Hazleton discovered that the bank robbers were in the bank, and they set up an ambush for the robbers when they came out.

Bun Smith, a.k.a. "Arizona Smith" had a boarding house on the main street. He was one of the guys who set up the ambush, along with the BC Provincial Police and some local citizens.

So the bank robbers were holed up in the bank, and Bun was firing at the robbers from the middle of the street behind a large boulder of silver ore that had been donated as a monument by a local mine. And the story goes that Bun ran out of bullets, so his wife walked across the street to him in plain sight, dropped a box of bullets beside him and walked away, and then the gunfire resumed. A newspaper story of the time says that over 500 rounds of ammunition were fired in the battle.

In the end they killed three of the guys, wounded and arrested three, but the leader got away with the loot.

And the story Dad told was that in the gunfight Bun was using the 44/40 that I still own. I have no idea if that was true. He certainly owned that rifle at that time. There was a rumour that there were two notches carved under the butt plate to note the two men Bun shot, but I took the butt plate off, and there's nothing there. Still, it makes a good story.

9.   *Amar Dev – The Mouli*

This story is about my childhood when I was just graduated from elementary school to Grade 6. There was I, maybe the second or third day in the Middle School and I'm feeling very independent, because Primary School was a lot of supervision, and my parents involved, and now I think I'm grown up and I can manage myself. Everything should be different.

I used to bicycle to my middle school, which was quite far. So after the second or third day they said I had to learn Sanskrit, which is similar to Latin in Europe, a very old language Many other languages came out if Sanskrit. But I knew that Sanskrit was not my thing, but I had to learn it.

So I go to this class, and I saw the teacher once in a while, walking back and forth to other classes. This was like a big guy, with a white complexion totally like a European, and he had a turban like one side sticking out, and the other side sticking to the back, one of those big turbans that big shots wear. The ones that want to show they are boss. Like he knows everything. And this was the Sanskrit teacher.

And there I am, a little guy, sitting in his class very quietly and very enthusiastic. You had to repeat a lot of things there, because they wanted you to remember things, you know, language you have to repeat things.

Hey rama, hey rameh, hey ramah – Present, future, past. At that time, I knew it.

All of a sudden he stopped the class. "Stop, stop, stop."

He said to me, "Come here."

So I go to him and I'm a little baffled. Why did he call me? All the students are looking. I was a little bit of a standout kind of guy. And everybody was thinking, "Oh, he's in trouble."

And he said, "Go get me a mouli." Mouli is a vegetable. He cut it and ate it with salt. That was his habit. He asked students to bring it.

So he asked me, and I was surprised. "Why did he ask me?" I'm mad inside. "Why did he call on me? I'm the only Sikh guy in the class, with a little bun on my hair. I didn't have a turban, just a bun. I was young at that time.

So I go, I pull up that mouli, and I look around here and there, and I said, "I have to give him a lesson, too." So I washed the mouli in the sewer line.

Then I thought "Okay, that will please me to give him some trouble, too." So I took the mouli back, smiling a little bit.

And he bit the mouli, and he smelled something. He stopped right there. "You washed this mouli?"

I said, "Yes."

"Where?"

I said, "In the tap."

He said, "Where?"

I said, "There."

He said, "Okay, show me the tap." He started walking.

I thought. "Now I'm in trouble." There was no tap. So I'm hoping there is a tap, but there is no tap.

He hit me, a slap on the face. I was really mad, but I didn't know what to do.

But he was wearing a lungi. I had seen lungis before. You tie it in the front and you tie in the back. So I knew how to open this lungi, right? So I go around behind him and I pull his lungi. I'm a little guy. I can't do any thing when he hit me. I can't do anything, but I'm really mad. So I pull his lungi and his lungi came down. You could see his underwear. Everyone was watching.

And then I ran. Huffing and puffing. What could I do?

I quickly went home and didn't tell anyone, because I'd get beaten again. My Dad was really strict about disrespecting people and all that. So I just kept quiet.

So the next day, waking up, "I don't feel like going to school." I'm pretending. But anyway, I had to go. There was nothing wrong with me, so they forced me to go to school.

So I went to the principal. "I can't go to his class. I'll go to any other class, but I can't go to his." All the students are looking at me like I'm a sheep. Now what will happen? They loved it. They were all smiling. Nobody was supporting me. Nobody came to me and said, "You did the right thing." Oh, man, that was making me more mad. I had no friends, nothing there.

So I finally go to the principal and tell him, this guy called me and I feel bad, I felt sick and that's why he called me, because he's a racist.

That worked very well. The principal agreed with me. He said, "Yes, I will investigate this. I will talk to him, son. Don't be afraid. Go to the other classes, okay? I'll tell the other teachers."

I felt a bit better. At least he allowed me to go to the other classes. So I went to the other class, and all the students are looking at me. "Oh, man, he escaped." They were hoping I'd be suspended, but nothing happened.

To cut the story short, after about seven days the principal called me and said, "You can go to his class. Shake hands with him, apologize that you did wrong, and he has apologized to me, that he shouldn't have called you. He realized that he made you mad. But you can go back.

I said, "No, I don't want to learn from him. He's going to beat me." I refused.

They said, "Well, what are you going to do?"

I said, "I'll study myself. You give me the lessons and whatever I can get from my friends, I'll learn." And I learned. I passed pretty well. I did the best in the class actually. Because I had to prove that I could do it.

That was in Rajistan.

10. Amar Dev – Riding Horses.

This is the same town, Sarchur. That time I was probably Grade 7. We used to live in an army barracks. My father was in the army. We used to go outside the city for weekends because my father was very respected and we had some Sikh friends and they were farmers with a lot of land, like 300, 500 acres. Well-to-do guys. So they became friendly with my father, and my father would take us to the farms. One of the farmers had a horse. As soon as I saw the horse, and an older guy was riding the horse. He had a big white mustache and a big turban, and a white beard and white clothes. A very good-looking gentleman. That was the children's grandfather. He came and he patted the horse, and they took the horse into the barn, and I'm just...I said, "This is it. I want to do it."

I told my father's friend, "I'd like to ride the horse."

"Oh, you like the horse?"

"Oh yeah, I do."

"Well, my kids, they don't like it. They hate it."

I said, "No, I like it. Can I do it?"

He said, "Why not? In the morning, you get ready, and I'll bring it. You can ride with me."

I said, "Okay."

So early in the morning I went with him, and I rode behind him, and we went, tik-tik, tik-tik, you know. We went all over.

A couple of times he asked me, "Are you tired?"

I said, "No, I want to ride alone on the horse."

He said, "How will I go? Walk?"

I said, "I don't know."

"Maybe tomorrow morning I'll bring the horse."

"Okay."

He said, "You sure?"

I said, "Sure."

He said, "Okay, I'll go with you and walk the horse."

To cut the story short, I ended up being a good student, and he was a very good guy, very supportive, and then I wanted the horse to run. It was an old horse, and he wouldn't run very fast, you know, tik-tik, tik-tik-tik-tik t-tik. And that was it.

But there was another guy, and he had a better horse, that could run a little bit better. It was a mule. So I started going to him, but he used to live right in the city.

So I said, "There I go. I don't have to go all the way to the farm, on weekends only." I wanted to ride more. So I made this guy a friend. They were hauling bricks on that mule. It was very strong. So I made friends with him. I said, "I want to ride, I'll help you with your work."

He was a nice guy, so he allowed me to ride the mule after work when the brick work was done. He was a very poor guy, in a shantytown, and I went there and took him buttermilk to drink and that sort of thing, so he was very happy to loan me his mule.

So I would go out of the city, and slowly and slowly I became a good horse rider. I could make the mule run.

So I declared to my parents, "I can ride horses really good. Oh, yeah, very good.

And they said, "Very good, yeah. Very good."

So we went on a holiday in Punjab. And there, my mother's sister lived close to the border with Pakistan. It's only 3-4 miles from there. So I tell them that I like horses, and I'd like to ride a horse. I'd heard they had horses in the village. So they brought a good horse for me. The guy came, but he said, "Man, this horse is a real devil. He won't stand. He's always moving around. So I'm a little bit scared."

He said, "You want to ride this horse, this is a naughty horse. You be careful."

I said, "I don't know."

So anyway, he's holding the reins of the horse and I jumped on, and I just kicked it, hey? Man, did that horse take off! The guy is still asking me if he should ride with me, but the horse takes off, and he's going.

I was just sticking on him. I had the idea. But there comes this little creek, and he tried to jump the creek, and I fell into the creek. I wasn't hurt. I got up and I looked around for somebody to help me. But the horse stopped. He didn't run away. So I slowly went to the horse and I patted him and climbed up again, and then the horse took off again, the same speed.

Anyway, now I'm in control. I know how to handle this guy.

But he stopped right at a wire fence. The India-Pakistan border. He stopped right there. And there was a border post, an army post. But nobody was there. So the horse stopped. I got down, and patted the horse and I tied him. I looked around, but there was nobody there, and I didn't know how to get back. So I waited.

Finally this farmer showed up. He said, "Where's the other guy? He's sending a kid today?"

I said, "Who's this guy?"

"The guy the horse belongs to. He comes here. You don't know? You're just a kid. You shouldn't be doing these things."

I said, "What are you talking about?"

He said, "He's a smuggler, don't you know that? He brings opium to me, here."

"Oh, man." I didn't understand too much. I just ignored it. I just said, "Yeah, yeah." I didn't tell him that the horse took off without permission. But anyway I said, "Now how do I go back?"

He said, "I don't know. You'll have to figure it out." But then he said, "There's another guy. Just wait."

Then the post guys came. The security guys. One guy with a rifle. And he said the same thing. "He's sending the kids, now." He thinks I'm smuggling.

I didn't understand, anyway. So I asked him, "Hey, listen, guy, I want to go back now."

"You just climb on the horse," he said. "He'll go back. Don't worry."

That's exactly what I did. I climbed back on the horse, but he wasn't running this time. He went slow, slow. It took me about an hour and a half. But I enjoyed it. I didn't want any more running. So I went back and the whole village was standing there. They thought I was finished, because I took so long, 2-3 hours.

So when I came back, they asked me a lot of questions. "Where did you go? What happened?"

I said, "I went to the police post."

"Oh you went there? Oh, no. I don't know anything."

My Dad was also mad with me. He said, "You see? Riding horses?"

After that, I wasn't so enthusiastic about riding horses.

11.   Amar Dev – Hunting Rabbits

This was in our home town of Dakota. My younger brother and I, he was in the navy cadets, and he came home and he said to me, "Oh, let's do something. There's nothing to do here. I'm bored. Let's go visit our Massi." Massi is my mother's sister, and they lived in a farm about 20-25 miles away. So we said we would bike it together.

So we started going together on the bike. He sat in the back. He was younger, I'm older, so I had to pedal. So we went about 5-6 miles outside the city limits, and there were these young guys with a nice, greyhound kind of dog. We saw him running around, and so we stopped, because we were tired. "Let's talk to these guys and find out what they were doing."

They said, "We are hunting rabbits." This was the month of April, harvest time, when all the beets were harvested and the fields were empty, and there was just the stubble, sticking up. And we were barefoot. I removed my shoes because it was too hot.

I said, "Can we help you guys?" I thought that, being a smarter guy, I could help them. The dog was good, but I could help.

So we ran after the rabbits. We ran and ran and ran, and finally the rabbit was tired, and it just sat there. The fields were bare, and he had nowhere to hide. So he just sat there and the dog came up and grabbed him. Then I got the rabbit from the dog.

The owner of the dog came up and said, "Give us the rabbit."

I said, "No, I caught the rabbit. Why should I give it to you?"

So there was going to be a fight erupting. My younger brother brought a stick and said, "Okay, I'm going to hit those guys."

I said, "No, no, don't do that. All the villagers are going to come and we'll be in big trouble. I'll make a deal with them."

I had a couple of rupees in my pocket, so I pulled out one rupee, and I said, "I'll give you one rupee, and you'll forget about it."

And they said, "Oh, sure." Because one rupee was good money in those days.

So I put the rabbit in my bag and off we went. When we were really close to the village, I got an idea. I said to my brother, "Say, listen. We are coming, and Massi is going to cook chicken for us today. We should save this rabbit for tomorrow when we go back to our village, and we can eat it there. Then we'll have meat for two days, rather than give it to Massi, and she'll cook it for us, and we'll lose the chicken."

He said, "Okay."

I said, "You better hold the rabbit, because they're going to hug me and shake my hand first, and you quickly hide the rabbit somewhere."

So that's what he does. He was about ten years old, my brother. As soon as I'm hugging and saying this and that he's going around behind, and I'm watching, and he went inside the back room. He hid the rabbit in where they put all the quilts. They have a pile of quilts in a big trunk. He opened that and he hid it there. He told me where, later.

So they had two kids our age, and they said, "Let's go fishing. We have a creek with good fish."

I said, "Okay, let's go fishing." So we were jumping in the creek. It was a beautiful place with lotus flowers and all that. And we're

83

fishing, but no fish. We spent two or three hours there and we came home, and the smell was so good from the pot. Massi was cooking something.

And I said to my brother, "See? My plan worked. Now we are getting chicken."

He said, "Yeah, you're right."

So we ate that chicken that night, and everything settled down. In the morning I said, "Okay, we should go now." We didn't tell our parents we had gone, so we had to go home in the early morning.

I said to my brother, "Go get the rabbit."

He went there and looked and looked, and no rabbit. He came to be slowly. "I can't find it."

I swore at him and said, "Go get the rabbit. You misplaced it." I was really the bossy type.

He was whining, "I dunno..."

I said, "Go get the rabbit."

He's saying, "No, no, I can't find it."

So I went myself, but I couldn't find it.

And my Massi asked, "What are you guys doing? What do you want?"

I said, "We have our bag."

"Oh, the bag with the rabbit? That's what I cooked last night. Didn't it smell good? It was good meat, right?"

We didn't answer. We were blank. We were thinking we were total bad guys, and they were asking again and again,

"You didn't like the meat?"

No answer. Finally we said, "Okay, goodbye."

Then, when we were leaving, Massi gave us some money. "Here's your bus fare."

I grabbed it quickly. Usually you're supposed to say, "No." Your parents teach you not to take it right away. You say, "No, no, no."

But this time I grabbed it right away. At least I got my rupee back!

12. *Jamie Long – A Hundred Fish*

I guess a lot of people probably might find it incredulous, but it was a factor of the time and the day and who we were as bein' young northern boys and whatever else.

There was this lake on the backside of Boo Mountain, which is Wolf Mountain in English. There was this lake that would freeze out, or run out of food for the fish in it, and there were a lot of fish in the lake, and the fish would be starving to death at the spring of the year before the ice would go out. And we'd go up there, and it was the best time to go fishing, because the trout would have roe in it, and you could use roe for bait and they would bite that like crazy.

We got up there, and I was kinda following a tradition of what Mikey Baduza and our eldest brother Sandy and Halvor Eidie and my brother Gordon did. They'd go up there and their goal was to catch a hundred fish.

I got ahold of young Dougie Montaldi; I met him in High School. We were 13 at the time, and we were going to go up there and catch this hundred fish. So we go up there and we walk the eight miles to the lake and chop a hole in the ice and get fishin'. Well, my gosh, it was just flippin' unbelievable. Those fish, you'd bait a hook, you'd stick it down the hole, you'd jerk your rod one or two times and you'd pull up a fish, and then you'd bait your hook and you'd do the same thing. In fact I caught two fish on no bait at all. I put it down there and I jerked it a couple of times and they bit on that, so you can understand the fish were starving to death. And we caught our hundred fish, and it didn't take all that long. We did it in the daylight, and it's wintertime. We only had about 5 or 6 hours of daylight, and we each had a hundred fish. So we're all happy about this. Of course we stayed up all night and ate fried bread and told ghost stories, all those things you do when you're a kid and you're camping out and you can't sleep because it's too darned cold anyway.

In the morning it's the springtime, we're talking about the end of March and it's high in the mountains and Burns Lake gets up to 13 feet of snow in the year, and there's a lot of snow on the ground. But luckily enough what happens is that in the spring of the year the top part heats up in the day when the sun comes on it, and then at night it freezes, so you've got great walking. You can go anywhere. It's the best time to be walking in the bush because it's just like a pathway wherever you want to go.

So that's fine, we start down the mountain, we're going downhill, and we're lucky, cause that's easier. These weren't big fish, maybe 12 or 14 inches maximum, but we still each had probably 30 pounds of fish on our backs.

Of course we didn't get started very early; it was about ten or eleven when we started down the mountain. Everything was great while it was cold, and definitely within the shade the crust would be there. But when we got out in the open area and it got closer to mid day, we started to break through. You'd step one or two or maybe

85

three times, and then you'd fall through. And then you'd step once, and you'd fall through again, and then you stand up, and hold yourself and kinda tippytoe, and then you'd walk a little farther, and down you'd go again, and then your next leg would go down.

It was exhausting. We had all that weight on, and it was killing us. Dougie was saying, "Oh, let's leave the fish. Let's leave the fish."

I said, "No, no, no, we can't leave the fish. My Dad will kill me if he finds out we did that. We can't do that."

And then I get a brainstorm. "Ah. I know what we'll do. We'll gut the fish."

So that's what we did. We sat there at the side of the trail and we gutted every darned fish. So all the fish were gutted, and I betcha we cut half the weight. And then we headed back down the mountain. By the time we got back we were late. It was six o'clock by the time we crawled in, very exhausted, but quite happy with our adventure of catching a hundred fish.

13.   Sandy Long – Winter of 68/69

Of course this is a famous story. I'm telling it.

It's probably verifiable in the records, but the winter of 68/69 in the north of BC and the whole north of Canada was extremely cold. We had seven weeks in which the temperature did not go above 0 Fahrenheit, -18 Celsius. Each night it was hitting -55 Fahrenheit or colder.

My job at that time was marking the right-of-way for a major road that was being built from Houston up to Babine Lake. Every day I'd go out with an erstwhile assistant and measure off from the established centre line to establish the clearing boundaries. It was so cold that when you went to tie the plastic flagging tape it was so brittle it would just explode. So we had to do a clove hitch, if you know what that is. You had to wrap the tape around the post and tuck it under. You couldn't just do a half-knot. You couldn't bend the ribbon any more than necessary, then you very carefully pulled on it and hoped it didn't break.

I can't remember how many assistants I went through that winter, but it must have been six or seven. I can name about five or six. They just couldn't put up with it.

But what did impress me, there was a young fellow about 18 or 19 years old that snowshoed from Takla Landing over Babine Lake to go to work at Topley Landing where we were camped. He was a Native kid, and I remember that the first day on the job he had moose tongue for his lunch. He was a bush Indian, and he knew his business. Many didn't, even in that era. They weren't that close to the land. But this young guy was well acquainted with cold weather. When it was so cold if you're experienced you don't stop to make a lunch fire, because you need to keep working, because you don't want to stop.

But it was so cold we just had to stop. Our lunches were frozen solid in the backs of our cruise vests on our backs, just frozen solid. So we did have to stop mid-day to warm up.

He taught me one thing that I still remember. I knew to make a seat of balsam boughs so you're sitting on boughs, but he said, "We're going to put those under our feet, not just sit on them." And sure enough, it stopped the loss of heat through the soles of our boots and kept our feet a bit warmer.

But we'd probably stop for half an hour or so and try to warm up a bit. But that was one tough show. We were on snowshoes, of course, but it was viciously cold. It would warm up to perhaps -30 during the day, and lots of the days that's as warm as it got. It was very, very cold.

But get this. The company was trying to clear right-of-way and burn the brush piles during this cold period. This was big corporation, gotta get the job done kind of stuff and it was completely stupid. We were trying to stay ahead of the dozers knocking down and piling the brush behind us. They were pretty good at keeping equipment going.

The weather was colder in those days. The winters were very, very cold.

That was a real test of employment dedication, I'll tell you, to be out there in that cold. I mean, I didn't mind it that much. It was okay; you just had to snowshoe hard, keep moving, keep working.

We marked right-of-way from Babine Lake south to not too far from the community of Perow where Highway 16 goes through towards Houston. It was quite an experience.

14.   *Sandy and Roberta Long – The House on 8th Avenue*

Sandy: We were recently married, just three months before.

Roberta: No, no no. We moved straight into that house.

Sandy: But the winter didn't start.

Roberta: The winter didn't start, but we have to start with the house. Sandy had rented this house before we got married.

Sandy: What a guy.

Roberta: It was on 8th avenue in Burns Lake. So when we came back from our honeymoon, we had our 68 Mustang full of stuff, and the back of your Dad's pickup with a table and chairs and one lamp that was a wedding present from Gran, and an old spring and mattress. And we moved into that house on 8th Avenue.

It was a shack that had been added onto.

Sandy: And it was owned by a landlord named Sonny Beck. He and his Mum had the hardware store in town, and they were...

Roberta: ...slum landlords

Sandy: Slum landlords, let me tell you. The house had been added onto...

Roberta: I was telling that part. And the addition had a basement, and the basement had 18 inches of water in it when we moved in that summer.

Sandy: And the level stayed the same all year, so it was pretty equitable.

Roberta: It was. So anyway, we just sort of ignored the basement and carried on. But on Thanksgiving weekend that year we went to Prince George, where we bought a Woods sleeping bag that we still use on our bed up at the cabin.

Eric: Ooh. Shameless product placement, there.

Roberta: And a dog. We got Snowy the dog, who was about a year old: half Lab, half Samoyed. We were looking for a Lab in a kennel, and I looked up and there was this white thing bouncing, and I said, "Let's look at that one."

So we brought the dog home and brought her into the house, and we're pulling stuff into the house from our shopping trip, and we hear, "Splash!" The dog is down in the basement.

Sandy: Swimming laps in the basement. She had an indoor pool.

So that was Sonny Beck's house. But then came the winter I described earlier, where the temperatures got very, very cold, and in fact, we had a skating rink in the basement. It was solid ice. In the corners of the living room there was frost maybe an inch or two thick along the wall. And we were trying to keep this place warm in the winter.

Roberta: You had to keep the taps running day and night.

Sandy: So anyway this happened on Christmas Eve it turned cold, and then seven weeks of continuous cold. But it was perhaps just after Christmas where the pivotal event happened, We knew we had to keep the kitchen tap running or we were dead. We were going to be frozen up. So we had the tap running. I think it was me, but

88

somebody turned the tap off in the evening. I think we had friends or relatives over, people at our place, and for one reason or the other automatically someone turned the tap of.

And we realized, "Omigawd, the tap's off."

So we turned it on. Nothing.

So underneath the house I go with a little propane torch, and it's cold down there. There's no insulation down there.

Roberta: The old part of the house. No basement.

Sandy: Just crawl space. And here's this copper line coming up out of the ground up into the kitchen where the sink was. So I started warming this up with the propane torch. And warming it up, and warming it up, and warming it up, and it wasn't getting any warmer, but nevertheless it was pretty obvious that the pipe wasn't getting too warm either.

Nevertheless, I heated it up too much in one place, and it went "Shhh," and it expanded up to twice its diameter, but it never broke. It went "Whoosh." It was steam pressure. I heated it too much in one place and not another.

So I went further up, further down, then further up, further down. Then all of a sudden it went clink-clink and we got water.

But the corollary to that story is that Ed Spanky the tugboat foreman that lived down Eighth Avenue but on the other side of the street had wood-stave water mains. If you were on our side of the street you had normal iron water mains, and they could hook an electric welder from one place to another, and thaw out the lines.

Roberta: We were on the new part of the street. The high-tech side.

Sandy: But on the other side they had wood stave water mains, and he never got water till June that year. The ground finally thawed out then. There was ten feet of frost in Burns Lake that winter. We came just that close to being frozen up too, and I just barely managed to get it thawed out.

Needless to say, we kept the tap running for the next six weeks.

I had that Mustang, brand new at the time, and it came out of the Coast and had no block heater. And it started every morning but one. I may have damaged the motor by doing it. But it had a high-compression motor, and it started at -55 in the morning. But oh, it was tough on people and equipment.

89

15.   Eric Long – My First Memory

I was born in Iran and lived there for 2 ½ years and the family moved to Canada and landed in Halifax and took the train across, I guess. I don't remember that. My first memories were in Houston, B. C. in Grandma and Grandpa's place, because there was snow.

Chris and I were going sledding, and one of Grandpa's big draft horses was chasing us down the hill, and I was freaked out. I remember that. And then I have a whole bunch of first memories, because they were building a house and everyone was living in the basement, because the basement was finished, and they were working on the upper part of the house.

Anyway I remember toddling up to Grandpa and he was sleeping, I guess I'd gotten up early. I remember staring, two inches from his face, and him opening his eyes, I remember blue eyes, and I remember his beard and stuff, but he woke up with a great big smile. I thought that was pretty cool.

Then that day I think I spilt the milk and I was really upset about it. I was trying to get the milk for myself, and I spilled it all over the table. That was all in that same, it's all jumbled up, it seems like it was part of the same memory.

Sandy: ...and the knife incident with Chris

Eric: I don't remember that.

16.   Amar Dev – First Job in Canada

This is about five days after I arrived in Prince George. My brother-in-law who applied for my immigration lived in Port Alberni. He asked me to stay in Port Alberni. He said, "Don't go to Prince George. It's too cold."

But somehow I learned that Prince George has snow. I loved snow. Watching snow and playing in the snow. So I declared that no way, I had to go to Prince George. And Harwant was interested, because she had a brother there.

So we were on the plane and I looked out and there was the snow. And I felt like jumping off the plane to play in the snow. Anyway, we came to the Prince George airport, and it was snow all over.

My brother-in-law's son Danny – I knew him from India – he came to receive us. He was so happy to see me and he said, "Oh, Uncle, now you came, we're going to have fun. It's really a lovely country."

And I'm out playing in the snow in my dress shoes.

90

So we went to his home, and after about a couple or three days another friend was working at Bear Lake at Polar Forest Products sawmill. He was a lumber grader there. He met me a couple of times at parties. When we first arrived, all the people who knew my brother-in-law invited us to their homes, and every day there was a party.

So he met me a couple of times. He was from a village very close to mine in India. He learned that I was an educated person and I came here. He said, "Oh, man, you came to the wrong place. There won't be any jobs for you, here."

I said, "Why?"

He said, "There's only sawmills here. There won't be anything else."

"Well," I said, "Why not? Maybe I can get a job in the sawmill. Maybe they'll hire me as a salesman or something."

He said, "Yeah, okay, get ready, I'll talk to my boss, and you get ready."

So he talked to his boss, and he said, "Bring him in."

The boss was really bad. So my friend came to pick me up for the night shift, around 6 o'clock. I was all dressed, in a tie and all that. My friend looked at me, he said, "Where are you going?"

I said, "With you."

He said, "Man, you're piling lumber there. You've got to be dressed like me. Take off all this jacket and tie. It's hard work. Now we'll see if your education helps you there." He was taunting me, like.

My brother-in-law said, "Yes, you have to go. There's no jobs for an education here. It's all labouring jobs. You made the wrong choice to come to Canada."

So he took me. I didn't have any good winter boots, or good gloves or anything. He introduced me to the manager. The manager didn't even bother to ask my name. "Just send him down there."

The night foreman just told my friend, "Just send him on the line there."

They thought I already knew the sawmill job.

There was a woman there, piling lumber. She was taller than me, and she was piling lumber there. And I'm ahead of her on the greenchain, and I'm supposed to pull some of the lumber off. And all the lumber is going to her, because I'm still trying to figure out which ones I'm supposed to pull. Finally she came to me, using really abusive language on me, saying, "Why the hell did you come here? You're making my life miserable." And stuff like that.

91

And all the lumber is coming left and right and piling up.

But they still weren't calling anybody. I said, "Why don't you call somebody, have them help us here." Because I had broken English. So I told her, "Call somebody! I can't do it. I don't know. Or you tell me what lumber to pull."

"Oh, you damn guy, pull anything you can pull." Anyway we had a big argument going on, and coffee time came along, and I was shivering with cold, and my feet were frozen. So I ran to the lunchroom and I warmed myself up. But then it's only ten minutes and they're going back and I'm still shivering.

So this woman came, and said, "Are you working, or not?"

I said, "Lady, excuse me, please. You find another person. I can't do it. The way you're doing it, I can't do it. You call somebody."

So they called the foreman, and he showed me the ones I was supposed to pull. He said, "You pull these."

So anyway, the night was over and my friend came and I said, "Why didn't you tell me how to do this job? Why did you bring me here and not tell me anything?"

"Okay, okay, tomorrow I'll tell you everything."

And the next day he showed me all the pictures in the book. "This is a 2 X 4, this is a 2 X 6, this is a 2 X 8"

I said, "Oh, okay." So the next day I went and I did better.

Most of the lumber was 2 X 4. So I told the lady, "Which one will you pull, which one shall I?"

She said, "Can you do 2 X 4?"

I said, "Okay, but I'll work after you. You do your job, and I'll do what's left." And I did it. I made a few mistakes, but I did it. The end of the day I was a good guy. She shook my hand and said, "Oh, you're smart. What happened to you?"

I said, "Yesterday was my first day in the mill. Today was my second. You watch me the third day."

The third day, I told her, "You sit down, I'll do the whole job." And she was happy. After the fifth day, I was the champion on the chain. I even removed my gloves and was doing it. The foreman came and he said, "Put your gloves on."

I said, "I like it like this."

He said, "No, no, if you're injured we're responsible."

So can you believe it, this guy who didn't know anything the first day, is removing his gloves and doing the job like an expert after 5 days.

There was a huge fire in the burner, and everybody ran to the fire. They called the firemen and they were spraying water. And they were all trying to put out the fire with big hoses. In my mind I am thinking, "I hope this fire burns the whole mill." Because I didn't want to work there, and if I go home and say the mill is still running and I'm not working, my wife and everybody will say, "He's a loser."

So the mill was half burned, so they told me there was no need to come the next week. All week, no need to work, and I'm happy. I'm putting my fingers under the tap, you know with warm water running for two or three hours every day, sitting in the hot tub. I'm thinking, "What did I do wrong here? This is a horrible place. How will I survive here? This is like an animal world. The people in the mill were total animals. Nobody talked sense. It was all abusive language. Everybody using the f-word in the van we used to go to the mill. They all talked nonsense like this. All of them hated the job. They're telling me, "Why are you working here? You're educated."

I said, "Why are you working here?"

They said, "Because we have no education, that's why we have to work here. But if you asked us, we'd quit right now."

Everybody hated the mill job.

The end of the story is that I came home, and after one week my friend called me and said, "Okay the mill is back to normal. They're running."

My heartbeat goes up. Now what do I do? I have no other job. I have to go. So we go together in the van. 5-6 guys and we go there. Soon as I go there my friend came to me and said, "Oh, the guy you were working for came back, so they don't need you."

"What? They don't need me, so why did they bring me here?"

"They didn't know."

I said, "What kind of rule is this? If this guy showed up, why didn't he tell them? What do I do now?"

"Oh, they'll send you. The trucks go back to town. They'll take you on the truck.'

There I am, no money, nothing. So they put me on the truck and he dropped me at the La Pas lumber mill on River Road. From there in the cold, like minus 34, I came to downtown. Then I rode the bus to where the bus driver says, "You have to put 25 cents in there."

I said. "I have no money."

So he said, "Get off."

Another bus driver came, so I jumped in, but this guy happened to be East Indian. He said, "Oh, you are Jeve Singh's brother-in-law?"

"Yes."

"Where did you come from?"

"From the mill."

"Why are you here?"

I said, "I don't know why I'm here, but I'll tell you later, but please take me." So he took me: no money or anything. That's it. The end of the story. I never went to the mill again.

(Ed. Note. Amar recently retired from a career as an engineer for the City of Prince George.)

17.   Harwant Dev – Our First Day in Canada

The first day we came to Canada, we landed in Victoria. We sent a telegram to my sister to pick us up. She lives in Port Alberni. But they didn't get the telegram. We got to Victoria, and we had no idea where we were going to go. So we took a taxi. My cousin lives in Victoria, and we had his address. So we told the driver to take us to his address. When we got to his house, there was nobody home. The neighbour came and told us that they both were working, and they'd be home around five o'clock. Now, we were only allowed to bring seven dollars each into Canada, and so we only had fourteen dollars in our pockets.

The taxi driver said, "Where are you going to go?"

Somehow I also had the address of my cousin's father-in-law. His name was Banta Singh. We didn't know where he lived.

I said, "Can we manage to have a taxi that far with the money we have?"

There was one guy walking with a turban. He had a brown grocery bag on his arm, and he was holding it and walking in front of us. Amar said, "Maybe he's Baltar Singh. Let's go ask him."

So we stopped the taxi and asked him. "Your name is Baltar Singh?"

He said, "Oh, no, I'm not Baltar Singh, but I'm his friend. Who are you guys, and how do you know him?"

We told him we were coming from India and we went to see our cousin but he's not home. And we don't know where to go. We don't know where Baltar Singh lives.

He said, "Well, I know. You guys get off the taxi and come to my house. They are all working, but in the evening I'll call them and they'll come and pick you up from my house.

Oh, we were so relieved. We asked the taxi driver, "How much do we have to pay?"

He said, "Thirteen dollars."

So we had one dollar left. It was a good thing he offered us to go to his house. So when we went to his house he offered us lunch and tea and everything. So by the time 5 o'clock came, he phoned my cousin. My cousin didn't have any idea we were coming to Canada. So when he phoned, my cousin said, "Which cousin? Ask her how she's related to me."

So anyway I told the man. I said, "Let me talk to him." So when I told him, oh, they all got so excited. Him and his brother and his wife, they all came to pick us up.

Our hosts were making tea for us, and my cousin said, "Let's go home now."

The host said, "We kept them all day, and now you don't even let them have tea." So we finished the tea and went to my cousin's house, and I phoned my sister from there. I said, "Hello."

She said, "Oh, are you leaving Delhi now?"

I said, "We are already in Victoria."

"What? How come you didn't inform us?"

I said, "We sent you the telegram."

"Oh, we didn't get any telegram."

The next day my cousin took us to Port Alberni from Victoria.

In the evening, while we were having dinner, the phone rang. They said, "Harwant Dev and Amar Dev are coming from Delhi, so-and-so time on this flight."

Anyway, it was a big relief for us to get to my sister's place.

18.   Jamie Long – Lost Children at Buck Flats

I don't even remember what year this was, but I'm going to ballpark it and say it was about 1979. I know I was working at the Equity Mine at that time. It was in the fall of the year, in October. I was working at Equity, putting in long hours. I got home on Thursday night.

Beverly says to me, "Did you hear about the little kids?"

I said, "What about the little kids?"

She said, "Two little kids went hunting up at Buck Flats."

"What do you mean went hunting?"

"Well, they were playing that they went hunting and they're only five and six years old, and they're missing."

I said, "Holy Cow, you're kiddin' me."

She says, "Yeah and there's a search party going on."

I said, "What I'll do is I'll saddle up Tango and I'll search with him. I can get more mileage riding Tango."

Tango was pretty green on the grass. He hadn't been ridden most of the summer, because I was working construction, right? So anyway I saddled him up and headed the 11 miles up there. I pretty well did him in on the ride up there. His hips didn't seem to be working too well. I got him up on the search and he just didn't make it. He'd had it. His back end was gone on him.

So anyway, I joined the search on foot, and we searched for Friday, and we never found anything. The little boys had a dog with them, and the dog hadn't come back then. I think the dog came back Saturday morning, but they couldn't get the dog to connect where the kids were, and then on the Sunday they found the one little boy, and he'd died. Then I think the Monday morning we found the second little boy.

This was Buck Flats, which was southeast of Houston, but I'd hooked up with a bunch of the Palling boys. I was with Ernie Neville, and a bunch like Ralph Lindaas, a core team of guys from Palling. What had happened that the RCMP had done this gridded zone that we were supposed to be following, and we boys from Palling said, "No. We don't think so. We're going to go up higher. We think the little kids are going to go upwards. Person who's lost is going to go upwards, not down. It's easier to go upwards than down. We're going to go up above.

So we went up above, way up above, and lo and behold, that's where we found the little guy, and our team was just behind the team that found him. So we were right in going up there.

What's weird about that is that the little boy that had died previous had fallen down a ravine and banged his head. The boys were wearing felt-pac boots and longjohns and winter coats, and they were well dressed to start with. When the little boy that died was found he had no clothes on at all, I think he was stark naked when he died. He died of exposure, of course.

The little guy that was found still alive had a wool sweater on, only, no bottoms and no boots.

I guess the thing is that you get lost and you're in a panic, you run, you get hot, and you stumble, you are messed up and you lose your boots or whatever else, and you just take it off and that's how you end up dying.

But anyway it was very, very sad, and we came back there, probably on the Sunday, I think it was just the weekend. They'd had a thousand people searching. They wrote it up in the Reader's Digest.

So I go back to pick up Tango, and they'd had the command centre where they coordinated it all in Duncan Gillespie's homestead where he was living.

I look back as I'm leaving and there's Duncan looking absolutely dejected, with a thousand paper cups all over his property that no one had picked up. Can you imagine?

I had a long, 11 miles to go back with a limping horse. I had to walk him because he was no good; I couldn't ride him. And I had to work the next day, so you can imagine how that was.

It was quite a deal.

19.   Nini Dev – When the Bear Won't Cooperate

This story is about my first summer, no it was my second summer working in the bush. The first summer I'd only done a few weeks, maybe a month, doing some tree planting, and at that time, I was oblivious. I'd never worked in the bush before. I was very naïve, and totally oblivious to bears or anything. I wasn't scared or anything, because I just didn't know.

So the first summer it was 1995, I was working with Mike Worrel planting trees. We were in a very remote spot, and worked very far apart. Fortunately nothing ever happened, and I never even thought about it.

So the next summer I was going to spend the entire summer working in the bush with my friend Jodie, who was one of my roommates at university, and neither of us was bush savvy at all. We had no experience. So this summer we were both going to be working on this road and learning all sorts of things, but this bear story is a little bit different from all the other things I had to learn.

So one of the days we started two lines. It was pretty early in the season. Eric wasn't there. He'd been there the day before. Each day, he'd say, "Oh, we forgot the bear spray again."

This kept happening for about the first week. "Oh. Do we have the bear spray? No, we forgot the bear spray."

But, again, I as so oblivious to bears I didn't even think to bring it. But the first day that Jodie and I were going to be on our own, we actually, luckily, remembered to bring the bear spray. It was the first day we had bear spray.

Eric: It was because we had bear encounters the day before. We ran into five different bears in the same day, on Sunday. And that Sunday I had to drive back to Prince George to go to work.

Nini: And we ended up seeing a whole bunch of bears.

Eric: you came nose-to-nose with one.

Nini: Wow, I am forgetting. Anyway, Erik was there and the bears didn't do anything. We threw rocks at them and they took off, so it didn't feel too threatening. But that did inspire me to carry bear spray the next day, because that was the first day Jodie and I were going to be all by ourselves.

So here we are tree planting along. We had a big cooler full of food: our lunch. We left it on the road and we walked up this hillside and we were planting there. So we're planting along, and part way through the day, all of a sudden I look up. "Oh! Bear. Bear, Bear, Bear!" I start shouting to get Jodie's attention.

It's probably about a hundred metres away at this point. It's pretty far. So we think, "Okay, you do all the stuff you read about and the bear's going to run away, and it's going to be good."

So we've got our tree-planting shovels, so we lift our shovels and start yelling at this thing, "Yeah! Get out of here!" and that sort of stuff.

And the bear just looks at us and starts walking down the hill towards us.

And I'm like. "Uh oh. What's on the next page? Nobody ever said this would happen, right?" It's always, "Make yourself big and yell and it'll go away." But we had no idea what you're supposed to do if it doesn't go away.

So anyhow, this bear is walking down the hill right towards us. At this point we're still yelling, but we're walking backwards down the hill away from it. But it carries on, walking steadily towards us.

Sandy: That was in Taylor. I was there, but not at that moment.

Nini: Yeah, you'd dropped us off, so we didn't have a vehicle or anything there. So we backed up, and I told Jodie, "Well, he probably wants our lunch. The cooler. That's what he's smelling."

The road is below us, and the bear's coming towards us, so he probably wants the lunch. Well, he can have the lunch. That's fine. So we kept going, and there was the lunch, and we think. "Okay, let's just get off this road."

Below the road was this gully and I remembered there was this house, way down below. So we thought, instead of staying on the road, because the road is going to be a long ways, let's go down this gully, and it'll be a shortcut down the hill.

Big mistake. Right when we get off the road and we walk into the bush you know it's a mistake, because all of a sudden it's swampy and it's thick and it's so brushy we can't even walk, and right when we get down the steep slope, Jodie falls into the water, into the swamp.

And I'm yelling, "Get Up!"

Because we could see the bear. Walk right past our cooler. Here we thought the bear was going to stop at the cooler and we'll take off, and the bear doesn't even look at the cooler. Just walks right on past it, right towards us.

So now we're in mega panic mode, because now it's like twenty metres away, and now we're in this swamp. And in our panicked moment we totally forgot, we're still carrying our tree planting bags. We're trying to get through this gully, and we've still got our bags slung around us.

So finally I'm like "Drop the bags!" So we finally got those off.

Now I'm dragging Jodie up, and then the other point I remembered, Eric gave us a little Cole's Notes on bears, after we'd seen the bears the day before, about bear behaviours and what you do and whatever. One of the things he said was predatory bears try to circle you.

Well, guess what this bear does next? It's trying to walk in a circle around us. So I remember this little tidbit. So I want to prevent it from walking in a circle. So if it went one way, we went sideways, to cut it off a little bit. So now it's bushy and tall grasses and stuff. This bear will kind of crouch down in the grass and watch us, then he starts continuing in this circle, and then he crouches again. And each time he circles, he's getting closer.

So, at this point I am very sure we are dead meat. We are gonna get attacked. So at this point, I start pleading with the bear. Now I'm telling the bear. "I just got married. You can't eat me. Don't eat me!" Because we just got married the week before, and I'm telling the bear this.

Sandy: Some bears are sensitive.

Eric: "Look, I still have my nail polish on!"

Nini: "I'm too young! I can't be mauled."

Yeah. So at this point the bear is close enough that we've got to use the bear spray. I never ever thought I'd have to use it, because you have to be so close to the bear to use it. But now I'm, "Okay, Bear Spray! Thank goodness we have it."

So I pulled out the bear spray. I got up on a stump, and hopefully this stuff's gonna work. We never actually practiced spraying it or anything, So I just "Kkshkshshkhshs" and emptied this bottle and sprayed and sprayed and sprayed.

At that point the bear's like, "Oh, I can't see anything." And he backs off.

Our plan was, while he couldn't see, we were going to scramble back up on the road and hopefully that's it, then we'll take off down the road.

And that's what happened. It was a steep embankment, and we didn't want to look back over it again in case he's right there, so we're kinda standing back on the road with our shovels, just waiting, in fight mode, to see if this thing's going to run up at attack us again.

We waited a few seconds, and nothing.

And then we just started running down the hill. And then we ran down to the house, and there was somebody home. We stayed down there and called Sandy.

You would think this was the end of our day. We'd be going home, right? But Sandy comes and we tell him our story, and he's "Well, that's nice. The bear's gone. Let's get back to work."

We had to go back.

Eric: I have a little story to go with this story. Specifically about spraying the bear. Nini didn't empty that full can of bear mace into the bear's face, because I took the can that she used, and I carried it for another seven years in the bush as a good luck charm.

Nini: I didn't know that!

Eric: I carried it every day. I had my regular bear spray. I'd never carried bear spray before these incidents. So after that I said, "Okay, it's probably a good idea to carry bear spray. And I'll carry the good luck charm, the one that actually sprayed a bear. Now I know that it must be good stuff."

Anyway, I carried this thing together with my real can, for years. And then, I dunno, I was getting a little less sentimental about it after a few years, and I was training a new crew at the consulting firm I worked at, and it came to bear awareness, and using bear spray, and we were getting the new staff to practice with canisters. We ran out of canisters. I went, "wait a minute. I've got this partly used canister. I've been packing this around for years. Probably doesn't work, though."

"KSHKSHKSH!" I spray it out in the air. The wind picks up and blows it into the crowd. Everyone's coughing.

Nini: High potency.

Sandy: And there's another corollary for that story. You went up to the Blueberry and had consistent bear problems all summer. Remember you took Shega out and she kept them at bay, but barely. It was getting to the point where they weren't even afraid of her. (Ed. Note: Sandy's German Shepherd cross, Shega, was a proven bear dog.)

Roberta: I don't know how you did that. I would have walked away.

20.   Amar Dev – A Ride-Hailing Bus in the Third World

They were supposed to take us to the International Terminal of the airport, but part way, they realized that there were more passengers who were going downtown, and the turnoff was before the airport. So they stopped. "Boom!"

They were taking our luggage off. They said, "Come down, come down."

I said, "What's going on?"

They didn't speak very good English so they couldn't explain.

I'm arguing. "What? Why are you doing this?"

All of a sudden "Boom." A taxi came. They said, "Go in the taxi. Go in the taxi," and they drove off.

So we got in the taxi to go to the airport.

(Ed. Note: Ride-hailing bus: a minivan that picks up many people going approximately the same place. Usually.)

21.   Amar Dev – Wrong-way Bus

This is a story from Malaysia. I took a bus. I had to go maybe two hours. It was 6 o'clock in the evening. From there, I had to take a ferry to go to Langkwi Island. The bus driver quickly loaded me up, "Go, go, go." He didn't ask me where I was going.

I just keptsaying, "I want to go to Chumfan"

"Go, go go."

"I'm on the VIP bus, a big double-decker. I sat in the top, and everybody was sleeping so I couldn't ask anyone what's going on there, where this bus is going. So I think, after two hours have gone by, I'll call the man to stop the bus. So two hours and nothing happened, and the bus is going full speed. So I come down and I bang on the driver's cab. He says. "Stay there. Keep sitting."

I said, "No." I keep banging.

Finally he opened up.

I said, "I was supposed to go to Chumwa."

He said, "Oh, it's past. It's back there."

So I said, "Let me off. I'll take the next bus back.

So he stopped the bus, unloaded my luggage, my backpack, "There you go." It was dark on the highway, and I'm all by myself. So I see a glimmer of light about half a kilometre away, on the other side.

So I walked there, and there was a guy working on a motorcycle. He was a bike mechanic. I talked to him. He spoke a little bit of English.

He said, "You falongi?" That means "foreigner" in their language. He said, "You falongi? What you do here? This very dangerous for you."

I said, "Well, I know. What can I do? They dropped me off here." So I said, "Any hotel here, where I can stay?"

"No, nothing. Just the highway. Big problem."

I said, "Where do you live?"

He said, "I live in the village, 2 or 3 miles away. I go on the motorbike, and I take my wife on the back. I have no room for you."

I said, "What'll I do?"

"There is a bus going from the other side, going the other way."

I tried to wave them down, but nobody stopped. "Vroom,vroom," nobody stopped; they all just went by.

Finally he came up with an idea. There is a police station a couple of kilometres away. He can take me on his motorbike, and I'll be fine. At least I can spend the night there.

He said, "Okay, come on."

So he took me to the police station. The police guy is sleeping inside. I can hear his snoring from outside.

We knocked on his door, and the guy said, "This guy is falongi and he can spend the night, and you can give him a ride about 10 km away, the bus station."

Oh, he was mad. He growls; he yells at me. "Get in."

So I go in and put my luggage there. So he went in, into the little room inside. There's a little room about two metres square with a bed where he sleeps.

And I'm sitting outside, in the reception area. And I start the fan, because there are so many mosquitoes there. Oh, the mosquitoes are killing me. And the fan goes, "Roaroaroaroarooop!" and it dropped out, hanging with only the wires from the ceiling.

The policeman goes running out. "What are you doing?" in his language.

I said, "Sorry, sorry, I don't know. I pressed the button and it started.

He says, "Okay, no, no, no more."

So the both of us help to put it back and wire it there.

So he goes back again, and he's sleeping again, and I'm sitting, and it's about 11:30, and there's the sound of music on the highway. And I hear some music playing, like a party kind of thing. "Oh, man," I said. "Sounds good to me. At least I can spend a couple of hours there."

So I cross the highway and go through the bushes, and there's a bar, a two-storey bar, and all these truckers sitting there and drinking. You go further and there's a truck stop. So all those truckers they come there and they're drinking beer and drinking whiskey. And they're fully drunk, all of them.

There are some girls, too. Four of them come, and they jump on me. Some on my back.

"Buy us beer, beer, beer." They wanted me to buy them beer.

The bartender came, and I said, "Do you have any place I can sleep?"

He said, "No, the only place to sleep is in a truck."

I said, "No, I don't want to go to a truck." So anyway I buy the girls beer, and they settle down a little bit, not bugging me.

Finally I can't stay there. They said, "Now we close at 2 o'clock." They start closing it down. They tell me, "Go, go, now." Then they say, "Where are you staying?"

I say, "The police station."

So I go back to the police station, and I try to sleep on the chair there, and I can't sleep. At 6 o'clock, he says, "Grrrhrrhrrrr get up, get up. The bus goes at 7 o'clock to the place where the ferry is, about ten kilometres away. I'll take you to the bus stop, the bus will take you to the ferry."

So he took me there. Oh, boy, when I got there it was a school bus, not a regular bus, and the bus is already full with the kids, because they go to school in the early morning.

So the bus driver said that the only place you can sit is on the top of the bus. There were no seats there.

So I climb up on the bus, and we go to the ferry stop, and that saved my life. When I told that story to some people, they said, "Man oh man, you're very lucky. There are so many robberies on that highway. They kill people there. How did you manage it? I can't believe it."

One of the foreigners told me that it's a very dangerous area for foreigners, especially if you don't speak the language.

22.   Eric Long – A Cultural Misunderstanding

We were on the bus in New Delhi. We had been touring in Rajistan, and we'd finished our tour, hitting some of the ancient tourist sites. I wish I remembered the names of them better. The astrological museum or whatever that was built by the man who built the Taj Mahal.

Anyway we were seeing these sites, and the usual thing, me being a not-pushy Canadian, all these bijis and bapajis (grannies and grandpas) would put their elbows up and get into the bus first, and be sitting at the back. Nini would sort of push her way in, too, and I'd be the last one to get on. Then I'd have to find a place to sit, which would be the last place, so we often weren't sitting together. Nini looked like a foreigner, but not the same kind of foreigner I was. So at some point, we were in different seats, and I was looking out the window and reading tourist books, and she was looking out the window reading different tourist books, figuring out what we were supposed to do. I recognized some sightseeing thing out the window. I leaned over a couple of seats and tapped her on the shoulder and said something. There was a big hum of rattle and people talking and whatever else, but I tapped her on the shoulder and was pointing at something. She nodded, and I sat back down, and a middle-aged Indian gentleman turned to me. He was sitting in front of me. He turned in his seat and puffed himself up and said, "You, sir, do not touch Indian girls. In India you do not touch girls like that."

And this was actually a little ways into the trip, because I was losing a little of my polite Canadian, and I'd kind of had enough of things like that, so I said, "Look, you can sit down, and you can stop talking. That's my wife, and I'm allowed to talk to her if I want to!"

It was a bit of an outburst. He started it, but I continued it, right? I kinda lost my temper, and I don't lose my temper. But anyway there were a lot of people that were kind of giggling at him. They thought it was pretty funny.

104

Book 3 Participants

For the safety of relatives and friends still living in their former countries, some of our storytellers have requested that their names be abbreviated or omitted.

1. Mohammed Abadullah

Mohammed (p. 29) is a student at Woodward Hill Elementary.

2. The Badayev Family: Alex Badayev, Olena Chemeris, Yuliya Badayeva

The Badayeva family emigrated from Ukraine in 2003. Alex (p. 64, 66, 70) is a businessman. Olena (p. 67, 74) works in Olympic Dairy, and Yuliya (p. 72) is finishing a BSc program at UBC.

3. Benjamin and Eva

I am from Mexico. My wife is Eva. Many, many years ago I lived in Mexico. My three children came to Canada. Only my wife and I were left in Mexico.

I said, "My three children. What happened? Please come back."

My wife answered, "It's okay, it's okay."

Our children said, "Come to Canada."

"Oh, Canada? Surprise. It is Beautiful." Mexico is okay, but Canada is better. (p. 31, 32)

4. Joan Campbell

I was born in 1919 in a tiny village called Chinnor in the Chiltern Hills in the south of England. My grandfather was a minister of the Church of England. My father died leading his men out of the trenches in WW I, so I grew up in my grandfather's rectory. (p. 41)

5. Dev Family: Amar, Harwant, Nini

The Dev family emigrated to B. C. from India in 1976. Amar (p. 77, 80, 82, 90, 101) is now retired from the Engineering Department of the City of Prince George, Harwant (p. 94) is a retired nurse, and Nini (p. 97)(married to Eric Long) is the Director of Highway Design and Survey Engineering for the Ministry of Highways and Infrastructure.

6. Allan Brown

I was born in 1932 in Willoughby, the next to youngest in a family of 10 children (two of them died very young). I was brought up in the logging business. I spent 20 years as a blaster, and I still have all my body parts! I retired to Sechelt, and now live across the hall from my brother in Langley Lodge. (p. 60)

7. Tom Brown

I was born in 1923 up in Willoughby, which is close to here, and I lived there until I was three years old, when we moved down to on 200th at the foot of the hill. In total we had 8 children in our family, four girls and four boys. I grew up when Dad was logging with horses, and I loved being out in the woods with the horses. I spent my life logging, building logging roads, and working on logging equipment. I was married for 69 years and raised 2 children. (p. 58, 59)

8. Brenda Casey

I was born in Winnipeg. My father came over after the Russian Revolution to Canada. My mother was born in Canada. I grew up in the north end of Winnipeg, which at the time was a very unique location in Canada in terms of ethnicity and variety and the style of life that people were making. It was the first middle class area that was formally designated as such.

I grew up with other children of immigrant families. Often both parents were immigrants although there were certainly enough people in the neighbourhood who were Canadian born and bred. It was an interesting mixture: different ethnicities and backgrounds. (p. 48)

9. Darryl Catton

I was born in Huntsville Ontario, and I lived there until I joined the Air Force when I was 17. I went to school there. I learned my trade in the Air Force, and I worked as a Stationary Engineer. (p. 42)

10. The Giles Family: Hal, Rosalyn.

Hal (p. 48, 52) and Roz (p. 55, 57) came to B. C. in 1966. Hal is a Registered Provincial Forester, retired from the Forest Service, and Roz is a retired church secretary.

11. Maggie Gooderham

Maggie was born in England in 1923. She joined the British Air Force during WW II and served in Egypt. Her first husband was an Air Force pilot who died in a plane crash. Her second husband was a Canadian doctor who brought her to this country. She died in May of this year at the age of 94. She had a wealth of wonderful stories from a full life, and she will be sadly missed. (p. 17)

12. Joanne Harris

I was born in January 1929 in northern Saskatchewan, near Melfort. I was the youngest of 8 children. I left there at 17 to start a career as a secretary and steno in Winnipeg and Montreal. I came to Vancouver in 1961, where I met my husband. We married in 1966 and moved to Tsawwassen, where I still live. (p. 43,45)

13. Jamilla

I am Jamilla. I have one boy and one girl. I came from Iraq in 2010. I am a citizen of Canada now. (p. 16)

14. Trace Johnston

Trace is a student at Surrey Centre Elementary. (p. 49)

15. Marg Kennet

Marg was born in 1943 in Victoria, and brought up there and on an orchard between Blind Bay and Sorrento on Shuswap Lake in the Okanagan. She was educated at UVic and UBC, worked as a Social Worker in British Columbia and is now retired and living in Tsawwassen. (p. 61)

16. Bernadette Law

I was born in Hong Kong. My mother gave birth to four children, all girls, and I was the youngest. I came to Canada to study Art at university, and have lived in Alberta and British Columbia ever since. I am a member of the Surrey Seniors' Planning Table. (p. 1, 23, 24)

17. Jack Lillico

Jack is a magician, salesman, mechanic and denturist, among his other interests. Now retired, he lives in Tsawwassen. (p. 45, 46, 47)

18. The Long Family: Sandy, Roberta, and Eric, Gordon, Jamie

The Longs were brought up in the 1950s in Palling, a farming community about half way across the province between Prince Rupert and the Alberta border. Their father was a homesteader, logger, and log home builder. Their mother was a school and piano teacher. Sandy (p. 26, 86, 87) is still logging and sawmilling in Prince George, Roberta (p. 87) is a retired high school and ESL teacher, Jamie (p. 84, 95) is a carpenter living in Nanaimo and working in the Oil Patch, Eric (p. 90, 104) (Sandy's son, married to Nini Dev) is a Registered Provincial Forester working as a Woodlands Manager for the Ministry of Forests, Lands, Natural Resources, and Rural Development, and Gordon (p. 75) has retired from teaching in Prince George to live in Tsawwassen and...edit this book.

19. Graham Mallett

Graham is a retired teacher and university professor who comes from Australia. He married Leda 1971 and has two daughters. He now lives Tsawwassen.

He is a 4th degree black belt and chief instructor of the Tsawwassen Shotokan Karate Club. (p.15, 26)

20. Kartar Singh Meet

I was born in India in 1941. I was the eldest boy in a family of 7 children. My father was in the British Indian Army. (p. 19, 20, 21, 23)

21. Jennifer Melville Roberts

I was born in 1930 in Sealchart, which is just outside of Sevenoaks, south of London. I came to Canada in 1956 and worked in bookkeeping and accounting until I retired and moved to Tsawwassen, where I live now. (p. 27)

22. Murguly Family: George, Sue

The Murgulys came to Canada separately as refugees with their families after the 1957 Hungarian Revolution. They met and married in Vancouver. George (p. 9) is a retired Engineering instructor from the College of New Caledonia, and Sue (p. 4, 6, 7, 9, 30) is a retired teacher from Prince George.

23. Mohammed Rafiq

My name is Mohammed Rafiq. I was born in India in 1945. My family migrated to Pakistan in 1949. We had to leave everything in India and walk all the way to Pakistan.

Then in 1969 I immigrated to Canada. I worked with the Ministry of Environment of British Columbia as an ecologist for almost 30 years and retired to Surrey in 2000. (p. 14, 18)

24. Roslyn Simon

Roslyn is a member of the Surrey Seniors' Planning Table. She was born and brought up in Trinidad, educated at Columbia University, and came to Canada in the late 1960s. (p. 1)

25. Harprincevir Singh

Prince is a student at Surrey Centre Elementary. (p. 16)

26. Deanna Vowles

As you might expect from reading her stories, Deanna has considerable experience in many areas of the performing arts. Her work with many singing groups throughout the Lower Mainland goes back 14 years. She has performed with 2 trios and a duo at various Lower Mainland venues. (p. 45)

27. Connor Wakelin

Connor is a student at Surrey Centre Elementary (p. 52)

28. Cal Whitehead

Cal was born in Canada, in Vancouver in 1926. After making several careers in Ontario, he returned to B. C. in 2001 to spend time with his mother. He died in May of this year, after contributing many stories, long and short, serious and not so serious, to the ElderStory Project. He will be sorely missed by all of us. (p. 34, 36)

29. Fay Whitehead

My name is Fay. My maiden name was duBois. My father came from Northern Ireland, so we're Huguenot descendants. Dad came to Canada when he was 16. I never did ask him why. He was the oldest boy in the family and why would he leave them? I'm curious about that now, and it's too late. (p. 37, 38, 39)

30. Anne Williams

I was born in the Netherlands in 1923. I came with my family to Winnipeg, Manitoba when I was about 3 years old. My father was a farmer. I was brought up on a farm. I married an airline pilot, and we lived in Winnipeg and raised 4 children. (p. 34)

31. Kendra Wilson

Kendra is a student at Surrey Centre Elementary. (p. 44)

ElderStory Committee

1) Gordon A. Long

Gordon is the recording technician, storytelling coach and editor of the ElderStory Project. He was born and raised in Palling, a small farming community near Burns Lake, B. C. He is a retired teacher, a playwright, director and acting teacher, and the self-published author of 9 novels. He has been a member of the Planning Table since 2011.

2) Judith McBride

Judith is the administrator of the Planning Table and the ElderStory Project. She was born in South London, England in the winter of 1949. She moved to Canada in 1974, settling in B.C in 1976. She has worked for the last 40 years in charitable & nonprofit endeavours.

3) Chanchal Sidhu

Chanchal is the Manager of Multicultural and Community Programs at DIVERSEcity Community Resources Society. She oversees a diverse portfolio of programs from settlement and integration to food security and seniors' initiatives. She has been a member and supporter of the Surrey Seniors' Planning Table since 2013.

The ElderStory Project

This project was conceived by the Planning Table, supported by DIVERSEcity, and funded by the New Horizons for Seniors program of the Government of Canada.

First we held recording sessions, for individuals and groups of storytellers in KinVillage in Tsawwassen, DIVERSEcity offices in Surrey, in Langley Lodge and in people's homes.

A second part involved our storytelling coach giving workshops in Woodward Hill and Surrey Centre elementary schools. At an evening storytelling session students, teachers and parents were then invited to tell their family stories.

Now the stories have been transcribed and will be made into a series of books.

Surrey Seniors' Planning Table

The Surrey Seniors' Planning table is an organization of seniors dedicated to connecting seniors with the community. We accomplish projects involving multicultural and multigenerational cooperation and try to enhance the lives of Seniors and promote an age-friendly community.

Other Planning Table members in the ElderStory Project:

Beverly-Jean Brunet	Bernadette Law
Luz Lopezdee	Kay Noonan
Mohammed Rafiq	Roslyn Simon
Evelyn Wallenborn	

DIVERSEcity

DIVERSEcity Community Resources Society, established in 1978, is a not-for-profit agency offering a wide range of services and programs to the culturally diverse communities of the lower mainland. DIVERSEcity prides itself on its well-founded expertise in assisting immigrants and new Canadians in their integration into their new community. Our programs continue to expand and change to reflect the unique needs of the diverse community we serve. We have a strong commitment to raising awareness of the economic and cultural contributions immigrants make to Canadian society, and to raising awareness of the value of diversity.

New Horizons for Seniors

The New Horizons for Seniors Program is a federal Grants and Contributions program that supports projects led or inspired by seniors who make a difference in the lives of others and in their communities. By supporting a variety of opportunities for seniors, the New Horizons for Seniors Program works to better the lives of all Canadians. Since its creation in 2004, the Program has helped seniors lead and participate in activities across the country.